EDITOR: Maryanne Blacker

FOOD EDITOR: Pamela Clark

DESIGN DIRECTOR: Neil Carlyle

. . .

ASSISTANT EDITOR: Judy Newman

ART DIRECTOR: Robbylee Phelan

DESIGNER: Lou McGeachie

. . .

ASSISTANT FOOD EDITORS: Jan Castorina, Karen Green

ASSOCIATE FOOD EDITOR: Enid Morrison

CHIEF HOME ECONOMIST: Kathy Wharton

HOME ECONOMISTS: Jon Allen, Jane Ash, Tikki Durrant, Sue Hipwell, Karen Hughes, Karen Maughan, Voula Mantzouridis, Alexandra McCowan, Louise Patniotis

STYLISTS: Rosemary De Santis, Carolyn Fienberg, Jacqui Hing, Anna Phillips

PHOTOGRAPHERS: Kevin Brown, Robert Clark, Andre Martin, Robert Taylor, Jon Waddy

EDITORIAL ASSISTANT: Elizabeth Gray

KITCHEN ASSISTANT: Amy Wong

. . .

NUTRITION CONSULTANTS: Isobel Brown, Kathy Usic

. . .

PUBLISHER: Richard Walsh

EDITOR-IN-CHIEF: Sandra Funnell

. . .

Produced by The Australian Women's Weekly
Home Library Division
Typeset by Photoset Computer Service Pty Ltd,
Sydney, Australia
Printed by Dai Nippon Co Ltd, Tokyo, Japan
Published by Australian Consolidated Press,
54 Park Street, Sydney
Distributed by Network Distribution Company,
54 Park Street, Sydney
Distributed in U.K. by Australian Consolidated Press (UK)
Ltd (0604) 760456. Distributed in New Zealand by Gordon
and Gotch (NZ) Ltd (09) 654 379. Distributed in Canada by
Whitecap Books Ltd (604) 980 9852. Distributed in South
Africa by Intermag (011) 493 3200.

. . .

Healthy Heart Cookbook.

Includes index.
ISBN 0 949892 66 1.

1. Low-fat diet — Recipes. 2. Low-cholesterol
diet — Recipes. (Series: Australian
Women's Weekly Home Library.)

641.5638

. . .

FRONT COVER: Buttermilk Pancakes with Golden Pears
(page 102). Plates from Studio-Haus. BACK COVER: Beef
and Pear with Garlic Mustard Sauce (page 72). LEFT:
Clockwise from back: Red Pepper Soup, Lentil Vegetable
Soup, Potato Zucchini Vichyssoise (page 10).

Healthy Heart Cookbook

ENDORSED BY THE NATIONAL HEART FOUNDATION OF AUSTRALIA

The wonderful food in this book can help your heart to be healthier and give you a bonus of energy and well-being. You can plan meals using recipes from several sections, plus enjoy a terrific lunch for 10 or an easy dinner party. Our recipes are so tasty, tempting and nutritious you'll never guess we've cut down on fat, a silent but serious trouble-maker for your heart and blood vessels. It's the fat you eat that can be transformed into cholesterol in your body, and it's vital to keep your cholesterol level down. Just by limiting your fat intake you begin to have control over your cholesterol. Now turn the page for the Heart Foundation's guide to eating for a healthy heart.

Pamela Clark

FOOD EDITOR

Eating for a

It makes delicious sense to take care of your body and avoid the foods it doesn't like. One of the main culprits is fat, and here's why.

What you eat is a powerful key to health. Your body wants to be well, but often your eating habits create problems that could be avoided. This is because some substances in food are changed by the body's chemistry into other substances which have undesirable effects.

Fat is one of those substances. It can be transformed into excess cholesterol. Too much cholesterol in the blood can narrow and block arteries, leading to heart disease. The amount of cholesterol you produce depends on several factors, but mostly on the type of fat you eat. Cholesterol levels vary from one person to another. It is all very complex and not yet fully understood.

3 MAJOR HEALTH RISKS
A raised level of cholesterol in the blood, along with high blood pressure and tobacco smoking, make up 3 major risk factors for heart disease. As your blood cholesterol increases, your chances of dying from heart disease go up accordingly.

With heart disease accounting for half the deaths in Australia, it would seem sensible to try to lower your risk.

The National Heart Foundation of Australia recommends that all adults should know their cholesterol level. A measurement of less than 5.5 millimoles (mmol) per litre of blood is desirable. (A millimole is the international unit of measurement for blood cholesterol.) A simple test in your doctor's surgery will reveal your cholesterol level.

The terms cholesterol, saturated fats, polyunsaturated fats and mono-unsaturated fats are often confusing.

CHOLESTEROL
Cholesterol has different sources. We all produce cholesterol naturally in our bodies; it is a white, fatty, waxy substance essential to life and is used, among other things, to make cell walls and hormones.

It is also found in all foods of animal origin such as meat, milk, butter, cheese, cream and eggs. It is believed that dietary cholesterol is less important than total fat intake in determining blood cholesterol levels.

SATURATED FATS
These are found mainly in animal foods such as butter, cream, milk, cheese, egg yolks, offal and meat. They are also found in cakes, chocolates, biscuits, crisps, ice-cream, chips and meat pies. Vegetable sources of saturated fats are coconut oil and palm oil in certain products made containing them. Check the labels.

Basically, when you eat these foods containing saturated fats, the body uses the fat to make cholesterol.

Some people make more cholesterol than others.

In our typical Aussie diet, we eat too much fat, particularly these saturated fats, which can result in raised blood cholesterol levels. Approximately half of us have a blood cholesterol level above 5.5mmol/litre.

POLYUNSATURATED FATS
These are found mostly in vegetable foods and polyunsaturated vegetable oils such as safflower, sunflower, maize or corn, soy bean and grape seed, and polyunsaturated margarine. These can't be eaten with abandon but can largely replace saturated fats. Walnuts and fish also contain polyunsaturated fats.

MONO-UNSATURATED FATS
These are found in foods including avocados, olives and peanuts, olive oil and peanut oil. They do not raise your cholesterol level but are high in kilojoules and should also be limited.

YOUR DAILY FAT INTAKE
According to the Heart Foundation, a reasonable total fat limit is approximately 90g daily for the average man, and 68g daily for the average woman, unless your doctor advises otherwise.

The average Aussie's diet consists of around 40% fat. If you follow our guidelines, you will be reducing that intake by a quarter; that is, your fat grams down to 30% of your diet. You can, of course, reduce it to a lot less than that with your doctor's guidance.

The Heart Foundation suggests a limit of 150g lean meat per serve. Meat should be trimmed of all visible fat, and allowance has been made for the varying percentage of fat which remains after trimming.

THE HEART SYMBOLS
The fat content of our recipes has been carefully calculated by the Heart Foundation, and the fat grams per portion are given at the end of each recipe. The heart symbols given below are a quick guide:

♥ ♥ ♥ = 5 grams and below
♥ ♥ = over 5 grams to 10 grams
♥ = more than 10 grams

As well, you can use the fat content chart to check some basic foods. A lot of fat is hidden in foods you buy, so it's worth checking labels.

HEALTHY HEART GUIDELINES
♥ Eat a wide variety of foods.
♥ Keep to a healthy weight; check with your doctor.
♥ Eat fewer fatty foods.
♥ Eat more bread, cereals, vegetables and fruits.
♥ Cut down salt intake.
♥ Drink less alcohol.
♥ Do not smoke.
♥ Exercise daily.

For more detailed information on cholesterol and heart disease, contact the Heart Foundation in your State.

Note: The figures at right show an averaged fat content of products. Variations will occur between brands.

healthy heart

APPROXIMATE FAT CONTENT PER 100 GRAMS OF FOOD

BEEF — uncooked, lean	Fat (g)
Blade steak	5
Chuck steak	2.9
Rump steak	3
Scotch fillet steak	4.4
Topside steak	3.2

BISCUITS, CAKES and PASTRIES

Biscuits, crispbread	6
savoury	16
sweet cream	24
sweet plain	9
Cake, plain	17
rich, fruit	11
Cheesecake	35
Fruit pie	16

BREAD and CEREALS

Bread, pocket	1.4
white	2
wholemeal	2
Breadcrumbs	4.4
Breakfast cereal; eg, Cornflakes, Weet-Bix	1
Flour, white	1.7
wholemeal	2.5
Muesli, natural	9
toasted	20
Pasta/noodles	1.3
Rice, brown	0.6
white	0.2
Rolled oats, uncooked	7.8
Unprocessed bran, wheat	6
oat	8.6
Wheatgerm	7

CONFECTIONERY

Boiled lollies	—
Chocolate, plain	31
Marshmallows (without coconut)	—

DAIRY FOODS

Butter	82
Buttermilk	2
Cheese, cheddar/tasty	33
cotto	11
creamed cottage	5.5
low-fat cottage	1
mozzarella, light/reduced-fat	19.2
parmesan	31.5
reduced-fat feta	14.5
reduced-fat ricotta	8.5
reduced-fat tasty	24
Cream, thickened (35% fat), 100ml	35
sour	35
sour light	18.5
Ice cream	6.5
Milk, full cream	4
reduced-fat	1.5
skim	—

Yogurt, full cream, plain or flavoured	4
skim/low fat, plain or flavoured	—

EGGS

Egg white mix	—
Eggs, white	—
whole	11
Scramblers	11.2

FRUIT

Avocado	22
Fruit, canned	—
dried	—
fresh	—
juice	—

LAMB — uncooked, lean

Chump chop	6.6
Fillet	3.6
Leg	2.2
Loin	3.9

NUTS — unroasted kernels

Almonds	54
Hazelnuts	36
Peanuts	49
Pecans	71
Pine nuts	51
Walnuts	52

OILS, FATS and DRESSINGS

Coleslaw dressing, light	4.5
Dripping, lard	100
Low-fat spread	40
Margarine, polyunsaturated	81
Mayonnaise, light	13
regular	49
Oil, olive	100
polyunsaturated	100
Salad dressings, French, Italian	37
low joule	—

PORK — lean

Bacon, untrimmed, grilled	35
Ham	5
Pork butterfly, uncooked	1
Pork fillet, uncooked	1.7
Pork medallion, uncooked	2.2

POULTRY and GAME — uncooked, lean

Chicken, breast	2.3
drumsticks, without skin	5
Quail	6.8
Rabbit	4
Turkey	2.2

SAUCES and SPREADS

Honey	—
Jam	—
Peanut butter	55
Soy sauce	—
Tomato paste	—
Tomato sauce	—
Vegemite	—

SEAFOOD — uncooked

Flathead	1.6
Leather jacket	0.7
Ling	2.1
Mullet	1.8
Mussels	2
Oysters	1
Redfish	1.8
Salmon, canned	5
smoked	5
Scallops	1
Tuna, canned in oil	22
canned in water/brine	3
Whiting	0.5

SMALLGOODS

Devon	19
Frankfurts	20
Salami	38
Sausages, beef, grilled	13
pork, grilled	24

TAKE-AWAY

Chicken, BBQ with skin	15
crumbed, fried	22
Fish, fried in batter	16
Fried rice	9
Hamburger, plain	10
Meat pie	14
Pizza	11
Sausage roll	14

VEAL — uncooked, lean

Chops	1.5
Steak	1.8

VEGETABLES

Chick peas	5.7
Lentils	1.1
Potato, chips	15
roast	5
Soy beans	5
Vegetables, canned	—
fresh	—
frozen	—

MISCELLANEOUS

Popcorn, plain	5
Potato crisps	34
Sugar	—
Tofu	5

Breakfast

♥ ♥ ♥

CITRUS COMPOTE

Recipe can be made a day ahead.

2 grapefruit, segmented
2 tangerines, segmented
2 oranges, segmented
¼ cup orange juice
2 teaspoons castor sugar
½ cup fresh mint leaves

Combine fruit in bowl. Add juice to sugar in pan, stir over low heat until sugar is dissolved. Blend or process juice mixture and mint until mint is finely chopped; pour over fruit. Serve topped with blanched strips of orange and lemon rind, if desired.
   Serves 2.

■ Not suitable to freeze.
■ Suitable to microwave.
▢ Total fat: Negligible.

♥ ♥ ♥

TOASTED MUESLI

Muesli can be refrigerated in an airtight container for several weeks.

1 cup rolled oats
¼ cup unprocessed bran
¼ cup chopped dried apricots
¼ cup chopped dried apples
2 tablespoons sultanas
1 tablespoon honey
1 tablespoon water
1 cup skim milk

Combine oats, bran and fruit in bowl, stir in combined honey and water. Spread mixture onto oven tray, bake in slow oven for about 45 minutes, or until toasted, stirring occasionally. Serve muesli with the milk.
   Serves 2.

▢ Not suitable to freeze.
■ Not suitable to microwave.
▢ Total fat: 9.7g.
■ Fat per serve: 4.8g.

♥ ♥ ♥

WHOLEMEAL RAISIN MUFFINS

Muffins can be made a day ahead.

¼ cup wholemeal plain flour
1½ teaspoons baking powder
¾ cup rolled oats
1 tablespoon honey
¼ cup finely chopped raisins
½ cup buttermilk
100g pouch Just White
   Egg White Mix

Combine sifted flour and baking powder, oats, honey and raisins in bowl. Stir in combined buttermilk and egg white mix; stir until just combined. Spoon mixture evenly into 8 holes of non-stick muffin pan, bake in moderately hot oven for about 25 minutes or until well browned.
   Makes 8.

▢ Suitable to freeze.
■ Not suitable to microwave.
▢ Total fat: 10.5g.
■ Fat per muffin: 1.3g.

RIGHT: From left: Wholemeal Raisin Muffins, Citrus Compote. Toasted Muesli.

Blue and white china from China Doll; cane tray from Keyhole Furniture

♥ ♥ ♥
WHOLEMEAL FRENCH TOAST

Make recipe just before serving.

4 slices wholemeal bread
1 tablespoon skim milk
3 egg whites
2 tablespoons chopped fresh parsley
4 green shallots, finely chopped

Cut rounds from bread using 9cm cutter; cut rounds in half. Dip halves into combined milk, egg whites, parsley and shallots. Cook in heated non-stick pan until lightly browned on both sides.
Serves 2.

◻ Not suitable to freeze.
◼ Not suitable to microwave.
◻ Total fat: 2.4g.
◼ Fat per serve: 1.2g.

♥ ♥ ♥
BUCKWHEAT PIKELETS WITH STEWED APPLE

Make recipe just before serving.

¼ cup buckwheat flour
¼ cup self-raising flour
1 tablespoon castor sugar
½ cup skim milk
1 teaspoon polyunsaturated oil
1 egg white
2 tablespoons low-fat plain yogurt
pinch cinnamon

STEWED APPLE
1 apple
¼ cup water
2 teaspoons castor sugar

Sift flours into bowl, stir in sugar, make well in centre. Combine milk, oil and egg white; gradually stir into flour to make a smooth batter.
Drop tablespoons of batter into heated non-stick pan, cook until bubbles appear, turn pikelets, brown on other side. Serve pikelets with apple and yogurt. Sprinkle lightly with cinnamon.
Stewed Apple: Peel, core and slice apple. Bring water and sugar to boil in pan, add apple; simmer, covered, until apple is just tender.
Serves 2.

◻ Not suitable to freeze.
◼ Not suitable to microwave.
◻ Total fat: 5.1g.
◼ Fat per serve: 2.5g.

♥ ♥ ♥
TOMATO MUSHROOM CUPS WITH BUTTERMILK DRESSING

Dressing can be made a day ahead. Make recipe just before serving.

6 large mushrooms
1 tomato, chopped

BUTTERMILK DRESSING
¼ cup buttermilk
1 green shallot, chopped
½ teaspoon grated lemon rind
2 teaspoons lemon juice
¼ teaspoon sugar
2 teaspoons skim milk powder

Fill mushrooms with tomato. Place mushrooms on oven tray, bake, uncovered, in moderately hot oven for about 10 minutes or until mushrooms are just tender. Serve mushrooms with buttermilk dressing.
Buttermilk Dressing: Combine all ingredients in bowl; refrigerate for several hours or overnight.
Serves 2.

- Not suitable to freeze.
- Suitable to microwave.
- Total fat: 1.1g.
- Fat per serve: Negligible.

LEFT: Clockwise from back left: Wholemeal French Toast, Tomato Mushroom Cups with Buttermilk Dressing, Buckwheat Pikelets with Stewed Apple.

China from China Doll; tray from Polain Interiors

♥ ♥ ♥

MANDARIN YOGURT CRUNCH

Make recipe close to serving.

1 cup low-fat plain yogurt
½ x 310g can mandarin segments,
drained
1 banana, sliced
2 teaspoons honey
TOPPING
2 tablespoons rolled oats
¼ teaspoon ground cinnamon
1 teaspoon honey

Combine yogurt, mandarins, banana
and honey in bowl, spoon into 2
serving dishes, sprinkle with topping.
Topping: Stir oats in pan over heat
until lightly toasted; cool. Combine
oats, cinnamon and honey in bowl.
Serves 2.

■ Not suitable to freeze.
■ Not suitable to microwave.
▢ Total fat: 2.1g.
■ Fat per serve: 1g.

♥ ♥ ♥

MINI SPINACH FRITTATA

Make recipe just before serving.

10 English spinach leaves
½ teaspoon olive oil
1 small onion, sliced
1 tablespoon water
pinch ground nutmeg
2 egg whites
2 tablespoons skim milk
½ teaspoon olive oil, extra

Boil, steam or microwave spinach until
tender, rinse under cold water; drain,
chop finely.
Heat oil in pan, add onion and water,
cover, cook until onion is soft.
Combine spinach, onion mixture,
nutmeg, egg whites and milk in bowl.
Lightly grease 4 egg rings with a
little of the extra oil. Add remaining
extra oil in non-stick pan, place egg
rings in pan, fill with egg mixture. Cook
until mixture is set, remove egg rings,
turn frittata, cook frittata until lightly
browned underneath.
Serves 2.

■ Not suitable to freeze.
■ Not suitable to microwave.
▢ Total fat: 4.5g.
■ Fat per serve: 2.2g.

♥ ♥ ♥

WHOLEMEAL ENGLISH MUFFINS

Muffins can be made 3 hours ahead.

15g compressed yeast
2 tablespoons warm water
1 teaspoon sugar
1 cup plain flour
1 cup wholemeal plain flour
1 teaspoon sugar, extra
⅔ cup skim milk, warmed
1 tablespoon cornmeal
1 tablespoon polyunsaturated
margarine

Combine yeast, water, sugar and
1 teaspoon of the plain flour in bowl,
cover, stand in warm place for about
10 minutes or until mixture is frothy.
Sift remaining flours into bowl, stir in
yeast mixture, extra sugar and milk;
mix to a firm dough. Knead dough on
lightly floured surface for about
7 minutes or until dough is smooth
and elastic.
Return dough to bowl, cover, stand
in warm place for about 45 minutes or
until dough doubles in size.
Knead dough on floured surface
until smooth. Divide dough into 8
portions, roll out each portion to an
8cm round. Dust both sides of rounds
with cornmeal, place on tray. Cover,
stand in warm place for about 20
minutes or until rounds double in size.
Cooks, covered, in non-stick frying
pan over low heat for about 10 minutes
each side or until lightly browned and
cooked through. Serve each muffin
with ½ teaspoon margarine.
Makes 8.

▢ Suitable to freeze.
■ Not suitable to microwave.
▢ Total fat: 24.4g.
■ Fat per muffin: 3g.

LEFT: Clockwise from back left:
Wholemeal English Muffins, Mandarin
Yogurt Crunch, Mini Spinach Frittata.

China from Villeroy & Boch

Snacks &

♥ ♥ ♥
LENTIL VEGETABLE SOUP

Soup can be made 2 days ahead.

1 teaspoon olive oil
1 clove garlic, crushed
1 small onion, chopped
2 small carrots, chopped
2 small sticks celery, chopped
½ cup brown lentils
3 cups water
½ small chicken stock cube,
   crumbled
1 bay leaf
½ x 410g can no-added-salt
   tomatoes
2 teaspoons no-added-salt
   tomato paste
1 tablespoon chopped fresh parsley

Heat oil in pan, add garlic, onion, carrots and celery, cook until onion is soft. Stir in lentils, water, stock cube, bay leaf, undrained crushed tomatoes and paste. Bring to boil, simmer, covered, for about 1½ hours or until lentils are soft. Discard bay leaf. Stir in parsley just before serving.
   Serves 2.
■ Suitable to freeze.
■ Suitable to microwave.
□ Total fat: 5.6g.
■ Fat per serve: 2.8g.

♥ ♥ ♥
POTATO ZUCCHINI VICHYSSOISE

Recipe can be made a day ahead.

½ small leek, sliced
1 potato, chopped
¾ cup water
½ small chicken stock cube,
   crumbled
1 bay leaf
¼ teaspoon cracked black
   peppercorns
1½ tablespoons buttermilk
ZUCCHINI SOUP
½ onion, chopped
4 zucchini, chopped
½ cup water
¼ small chicken stock cube,
   crumbled

Combine leek, potato, water, stock cube, bay leaf and peppercorns in pan. Bring to boil; simmer, covered, for

Lunches

about 20 minutes or until vegetables are soft. Discard bay leaf, cool slightly. Blend or process vegetable mixture with buttermilk until smooth; strain.

Pour this soup and following zucchini soup into separate jugs, pour simultaneously into serving bowls. Pull skewer through both soups for a marbled effect.

Zucchini Soup: Combine onion, zucchini, water and stock cube in pan, bring to boil, simmer, covered, for about 20 minutes or until zucchini is soft. Cool slightly. Blend or process mixture until smooth.

Serves 2.
- Not suitable to freeze.
- Suitable to microwave.
- Total fat: Negligible.

♥ ♥ ♥
RED PEPPER SOUP

Soup can be made 2 days ahead.

1 large red pepper, halved
½ teaspoon olive oil
1 small onion, chopped
2 cups water
½ x 250ml carton vegetable juice
½ small chicken stock cube,
**   crumbled**
½ teaspoon sugar
¼ cup low-fat plain yogurt

Cook pepper, skin side up, under hot grill until skin blisters; peel away skin and chop pepper.

Heat oil in pan, add onion and pepper, cook until onion is soft. Stir in water, juice and stock cube, bring to boil, simmer, covered, for about 20 minutes or until pepper is soft.

Blend or process mixture until smooth, return to pan, stir in sugar. Stir until heated through, serve soup with yogurt.

Serves 2.
- Not suitable to freeze.
- Suitable to microwave.
- Total fat: 2.3g.
- Fat per serve: 1.2g.

LEFT: Clockwise from back: Red Pepper Soup, Lentil Vegetable Soup, Potato Zucchini Vichyssoise.

Bowls and table from Corso de Fiori

FELAFEL WITH TOMATO CORIANDER SAUCE

Recipe can be made a day ahead.

1 cup (100g) dried chick peas
½ onion, chopped
1 clove garlic, crushed
2 tablespoons chopped fresh
coriander
½ teaspoon ground cumin
½ teaspoon garam masala
¼ teaspoon turmeric
2 teaspoons low-fat plain yogurt
1 egg white
1 cup shredded lettuce
2 wholemeal pita pocket breads
TOMATO CORIANDER SAUCE
2 teaspoons cornflour
1 cup water
1 tablespoon no-added-salt
tomato paste
1 clove garlic, crushed
1 tablespoon chopped fresh
coriander
2 tablespoons sultanas

Cover peas with cold water in bowl, stand overnight; drain.

Cover peas with water in pan, bring to boil; simmer, uncovered, for about 1 hour or until peas are soft. Drain peas, rinse under cold water; drain again.

Blend or process peas, onion, garlic, coriander, spices, yogurt and egg white until smooth. Spread mixture evenly into lamington pan, then turn out on lightly floured surface.

Cut into 20 rounds using 4cm cutter. Place rounds on baking paper-covered oven tray, refrigerate for 20 minutes. Bake felafel in moderate oven for about 20 minutes or until lightly brown. Serve felafel with lettuce in pocket breads topped with sauce.

Tomato Coriander Sauce: Blend cornflour with water, paste and garlic in pan. Stir over heat until mixture boils and thickens. Add coriander and sultanas.

Serves 2.
- Not suitable to freeze.
- Not suitable to microwave.
- Total fat: 7g.
- Fat per serve: 3.5g.

CURRIED CHICKEN AND PASTA SALAD

Recipe can be made 3 hours ahead.

2 cups (150g) pasta spirals
½ x 450g can crushed pineapple
125g chicken breast fillet
75g mushrooms, sliced
2 green shallots, chopped
1 tablespoon chopped fresh mint
2 lettuce leaves
DRESSING
1 teaspoon curry powder
¼ cup lemon juice
1 teaspoon polyunsaturated oil

Add pasta gradually to large pan of boiling water; boil, uncovered, until just tender. Drain, rinse under cold water, drain well.

Drain pineapple, reserve 1 tablespoon syrup. Poach, steam or microwave chicken until tender. Cool, cut chicken into slices.

Combine pasta, pineapple, chicken, mushrooms, shallots and mint in bowl. Add dressing, toss well; spoon into lettuce leaves just before serving.

Dressing: Combine all ingredients with reserved pineapple syrup in bowl.

Serves 2.
- Not suitable to freeze.
- Suitable to microwave.
- Total fat: 9.4g.
- Fat per serve: 4.7g.

ABOVE: Saucy Chicken Stir-Fry with Noodles.
LEFT: From top: Curried Chicken and Pasta Salad, Felafel with Tomato Coriander Sauce.

Above: Plates from The Australian East India Co.
Left: Tiles from Northbridge Ceramic and Marble Centre

SAUCY CHICKEN STIR-FRY WITH NOODLES

Make recipe just before serving.

160g chicken breast fillet
2 teaspoons olive oil
1 clove garlic, crushed
1 teaspoon chopped fresh ginger
1 teaspoon sambal oelek
½ teaspoon curry powder
1 red pepper, chopped
250g packet fresh egg noodles
1 cup shredded cabbage
4 green shallots, chopped
½ teaspoon cornflour
¼ cup water
1 tablespoon salt-reduced soy sauce

Poach, steam or microwave chicken until tender; cool, cut into strips.

Heat oil in pan, add garlic, ginger, sambal oelek and curry powder; cook until fragrant. Add pepper, noodles, cabbage, shallots and chicken; stir-fry until heated through. Stir in blended cornflour, water and sauce, stir until mixture boils and thickens.

Serves 2.
- Not suitable to freeze.
- Not suitable to microwave.
- Total fat: 16g.
- Fat per serve: 8g.

♥ ♥ ♥
CRUNCHY CARAWAY CRACKERS

Crackers can be made a week ahead.

¾ cup wholemeal plain flour
1½ tablespoons cornflour
2 teaspoons skim milk powder
2 tablespoons cornmeal
¼ cup rolled oats
½ teaspoon caraway seeds
1 tablespoon low-fat plain yogurt
¼ cup water, approximately

Sift flours, milk powder and cornmeal into bowl, stir in oats and seeds, make well in centre. Stir in yogurt and enough water to mix to a firm dough. Knead dough gently on lightly floured surface until smooth. Roll out on lightly floured surface to 2mm thick; prick all over with fork.

Cut rounds from dough using 4cm fluted cutter, place on ungreased oven trays; bake in moderate oven for about 20 minutes or until lightly brown and crisp. Cool crackers on wire racks.

Makes about 36.
■ Suitable to freeze.
■ Not suitable to microwave.
□ Total fat: 4.9g.
■ Fat per cracker: Negligible.

♥ ♥ ♥
CHUNKY CHEESE DIP

Dip can be made several hours ahead.

250g carton low-fat cottage cheese
½ small stick celery, chopped
½ small carrot, chopped
½ small red pepper, chopped
1 green shallot, chopped
1 small tomato, chopped
½ small green cucumber, chopped
1 tablespoon chopped fresh parsley

Combine all ingredients in bowl. Serve with fresh vegetables and crackers, if desired.

Serves 2.
■ Not suitable to freeze.
□ Total fat: 2.5g.
■ Fat per serve: 1.2g.

RIGHT: Centre: Chunky Cheese Dip; right: Crunchy Caraway Crackers.

♥ ♥

RICOTTA SPINACH GNOCCHI WITH CARROT SAUCE

Cook gnocchi just before serving. Sauce can be made a day ahead.

1 small potato
10 English spinach leaves, chopped
150g reduced-fat ricotta cheese
1 cup plain flour
CARROT SAUCE
1 teaspoon polyunsaturated margarine
½ small onion, chopped
1 carrot, chopped
1 cup water
½ small vegetable stock cube, crumbled
1 teaspoon no-added-salt tomato paste
1 teaspoon cornflour
2 teaspoons water, extra

Boil, steam or microwave potato until soft; drain, cool. Press potato through sieve into bowl, add spinach and cheese; mix well.

Knead in sifted flour ¼ cup at a time. Knead dough on lightly floured surface until smooth; shape dough into small balls. Place a ball of mixture into palm of hand, press floured prongs of fork to make an indentation. Repeat with remaining balls of dough.

Add gnocchi to pan of boiling water, boil for about 2 minutes or until gnocchi float to the surface; drain; keep warm. Serve gnocchi with sauce.

Carrot Sauce: Heat margarine in pan, add onion, cook until soft. Add carrot, water, stock cube and paste. Bring to boil, cover, simmer until carrot is soft. Blend or process carrot mixture until smooth, return to clean pan. Stir in blended cornflour and extra water, stir over heat until mixture boils and thickens slightly.

Serves 2.
- Gnocchi suitable to freeze.
- Not suitable to microwave.
- Total fat: 19.2g.
- Fat per serve: 9.6g.

♥ ♥

VEGETABLE FRIED RICE

Recipe can be made 3 hours ahead.

100g sachet Scramblers, lightly beaten
1 onion, chopped
1 clove garlic, crushed
1 teaspoon grated fresh ginger
2 tablespoons water
2 carrots, grated
½ small red pepper
3 zucchini, grated
1 stick celery, thinly sliced
1 cup cooked rice
2 tablespoons salt-reduced soy sauce

Cook Scramblers in heated non-stick pan until set, remove from pan; chop. Combine onion, garlic, ginger and water in pan, cook over heat until onion is soft. Add carrots, pepper, zucchini and celery, cook for 2 minutes. Stir in rice, sauce and chopped omelet, stir over heat until heated through.

Serves 2.
- Not suitable to freeze.
- Suitable to microwave.
- Total fat: 11.2g.
- Fat per serve: 5.6g.

♥ ♥

HERBED POTATOES

Make recipe just before serving.

3 large potatoes
¼ teaspoon paprika
FILLING
1 small carrot, chopped
75g broccoli, chopped
150g reduced-fat ricotta cheese
1 tablespoon chopped fresh chives

Scrub and dry potatoes. Prick potatoes all over with a skewer, bake in moderate oven for 1 hour.

Cut potatoes in half, scoop out flesh leaving 1cm shell; reserve flesh.

Place shells on oven tray, bake in hot oven for 10 minutes. Spoon filling into shells, sprinkle with paprika. Bake in moderate oven for about 15 minutes or until hot.

Filling: Boil, steam or microwave carrot and broccoli until soft; drain. Beat cheese in small bowl until smooth, stir in potato flesh, carrot mixture and chives.

Serves 2.
- Not suitable to freeze.
- Not suitable to microwave.
- Total fat: 12.8g.
- Fat per serve: 6.4g.

LEFT: Clockwise from front: Ricotta Spinach Gnocchi with Carrot Sauce, Herbed Potatoes, Vegetable Fried Rice.

Dishes from The Australian East India Co.; napkin from The Bay Tree

♥ ♥ ♥

JELLIED GAZPACHO WITH PAPRIKA BREAD WEDGES

Recipe is best made a day ahead.

430g can chicken consomme
¼ teaspoon tabasco sauce
1 tablespoon no-added-salt
tomato sauce
¼ cup tomato puree
½ carrot, chopped
½ cucumber, chopped
¼ red pepper, chopped
½ stick celery, chopped
½ tomato, chopped
½ teaspoon sugar
1 tablespoon chopped fresh parsley
1 tablespoon gelatine
¼ cup water
1 lettuce leaf, shredded
2 teaspoons low-fat plain yogurt
2 black olives

PAPRIKA BREAD WEDGES
1 wholemeal pocket bread
2 teaspoons water
1 teaspoon paprika

Combine consomme, tabasco, sauce and puree in pan; bring to boil. Stir in carrot, cucumber, pepper, celery, tomato and sugar, bring to boil, simmer, uncovered, 5 minutes. Remove from heat, stir in parsley; cool.

Sprinkle gelatine over water in cup, stand in small pan of simmering water, stir until dissolved. Stir into vegetable mixture. Spoon mixture into 2 wetted moulds (1 cup capacity), refrigerate until set. Turn moulds on to plates, serve with paprika bread wedges, lettuce, yogurt and olives.

Paprika Bread Wedges: Cut pocket bread into 16 wedges. Brush each wedge with the water, sprinkle with paprika, place on oven tray, bake in moderate oven for about 15 minutes or until lightly browned and crisp.

Serves 2.
- ■ Not suitable to freeze.
- ■ Not suitable to microwave.
- □ Total fat: Negligible.

♥ ♥

PUMPKIN TIMBALES WITH HERBED FLAT BREAD

Make recipe close to serving time.

250g butternut pumpkin, chopped
2 teaspoons polyunsaturated
margarine
1 small onion, chopped
1½ tablespoons wholemeal
plain flour
2 egg whites, lightly beaten
½ vegetable stock cube, crumbled
1½ tablespoons grated parmesan
cheese

HERBED FLAT BREAD
¾ cup wholemeal plain flour
2 teaspoons chopped fresh parsley
2 teaspoons chopped fresh basil
2 teaspoons chopped fresh
rosemary
½ teaspoon polyunsaturated
margarine
¼ cup low-fat plain yogurt
2 tablespoons water, approximately

Boil, steam or microwave pumpkin until tender; drain.

Heat margarine in pan, add onion, cook until soft. Stir in flour, cook for 1 minute, transfer mixture to bowl. Blend or process pumpkin until smooth, stir into onion mixture with egg whites, stock cube and cheese.

Pour mixture into 2 lightly greased moulds (½ cup capacity), cover with foil. Place moulds in baking dish, pour in enough boiling water to come half way up sides of moulds. Bake in moderately slow oven for about 45 minutes or until set. Turn moulds onto plates, serve with herbed flat bread.

Herbed Flat Bread: Combine sifted flour, herbs and margarine in bowl, stir in yogurt with enough water to make a soft dough. Knead dough on lightly floured surface until smooth and elastic. Cut into 4 portions, knead each portion well. Roll each into a thin round, cook in heated non-stick pan until golden brown patches appear underneath, turn and cook other side until golden brown.

Serves 2.
- ■ Not suitable to freeze.
- ■ Not suitable to microwave.
- □ Total fat: 19g.
- ■ Fat per serve: 9.5g.

LEFT: Pumpkin Timbales with Herbed Flat Bread.
RIGHT: Jellied Gazpacho with Paprika Bread Wedges.

Right: China from Shop 3, Balmain; plant from Liquidamber Nursery

♥ ♥ ♥
CARROT ZUCCHINI PIKELETS

Pikelets can be made 3 hours ahead.

2 green shallots, chopped
1 small carrot, grated
1 small zucchini, grated
¼ cup white self-raising flour
¼ cup wholemeal self-raising flour
2 teaspoons castor sugar
⅓ cup skim milk
1 egg white
2 teaspoons polyunsaturated
** margarine**

Cook shallots, carrot and zucchini in non-stick pan for about 5 minutes or until shallots are soft; cool.

Sift flours into bowl; stir in sugar, milk, egg white and shallot mixture. Drop tablespoons of mixture into heated non-stick pan; cook until bubbles appear; turn pikelets, brown on other side. Spread lightly with margarine before serving.

Makes 8.

■ Not suitable to freeze.
■ Not suitable to microwave.
■ Total fat: 10.5g.
■ Fat per pikelet: 1.3g.

♥ ♥ ♥
POTATO SALAD ROLLS

Recipe can be made 3 hours ahead.

12 large lettuce leaves
1 potato, chopped
2 green shallots, chopped
1 tablespoon chopped fresh mint
1 tablespoon chopped fresh chives
40g reduced-fat ricotta cheese
1 teaspoon honey
2 teaspoons low-fat plain yogurt

Cover lettuce leaves with boiling water in bowl; stand 1 minute. Drain, rinse leaves in iced water; drain on absorbent paper. Boil, steam or microwave potato until just tender.

Combine shallots, mint, chives, cheese, honey and yogurt in bowl; stir in potato. Divide mixture between lettuce leaves, fold in sides, roll up tightly to enclose filling.

Makes 12.
■ Not suitable to freeze.
■ Total fat: 3.4g.
■ Fat per serve: Negligible.

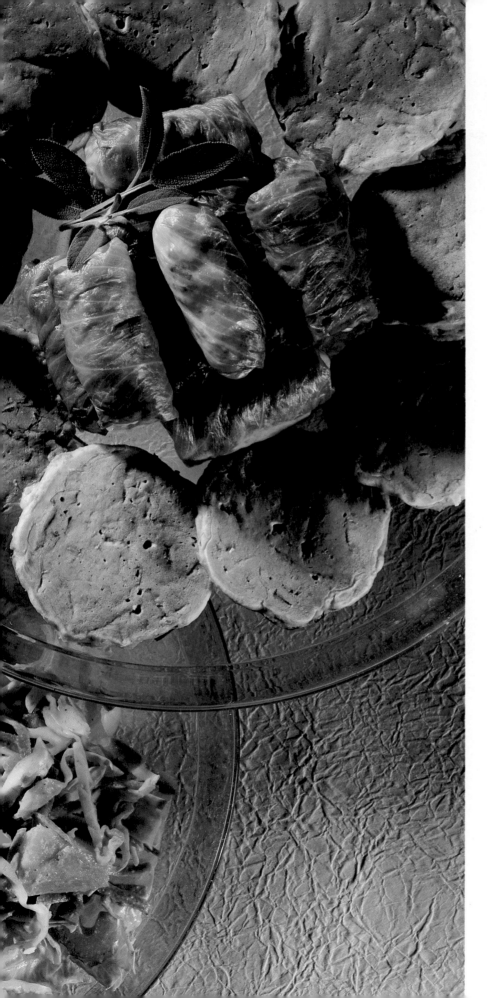

♥ ♥ ♥
CURRIED COLESLAW CUPS

Make recipe just before serving.

1 cup shredded cabbage
1 green shallot, chopped
1 stick celery, chopped
1 small carrot, grated
⅓ cup canned drained pineapple
   pieces
2 lettuce leaves
CURRY DRESSING
¼ cup low-fat plain yogurt
½ teaspoon curry powder
2 teaspoons white vinegar

Combine cabbage, shallot, celery, carrot and pineapple in bowl. Add dressing; toss well. Spoon mixture into lettuce leaves.
Curry Dressing: Combine all ingredients in bowl; mix well.
   Serves 2.
■ Not suitable to freeze.
■ Total fat: Negligible.

LEFT: From top: Carrot Zucchini Pikelets, Potato Salad Rolls, Curried Coleslaw Cups.

Plates from The Bay Tree

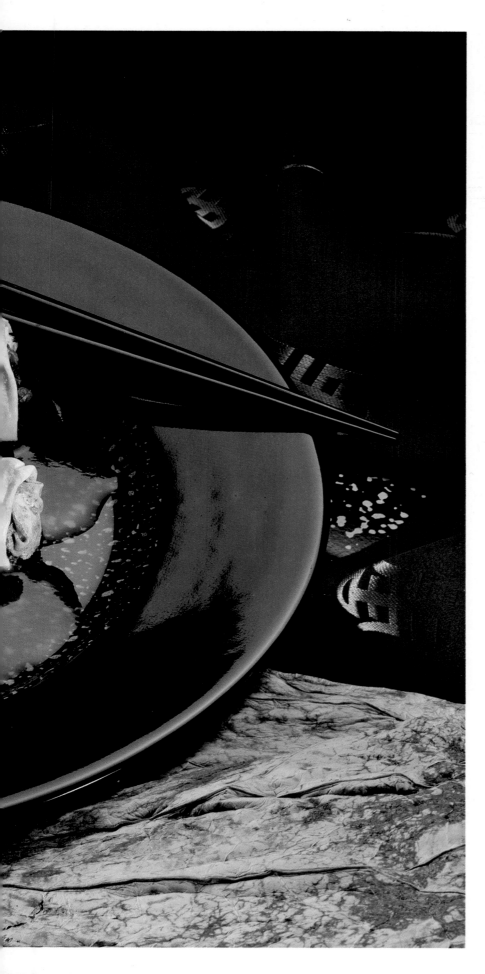

♥ ♥ ♥
VEGETARIAN SPRING ROLLS WITH SWEET AND SOUR SAUCE

Recipe can be prepared 3 hours ahead.

1 teaspoon polyunsaturated oil
1 clove garlic, crushed
50g mushrooms, chopped
2 green shallots, chopped
¼ red pepper, chopped
2 cups shredded Chinese cabbage
2 teaspoons water
2 teaspoons salt-reduced soy sauce
¼ small chicken stock cube,
  crumbled
1 tablespoon cornflour
6 spring roll wrappers
1 egg white, lightly beaten
SWEET AND SOUR SAUCE
½ cup pineapple juice
2 tablespoons white vinegar
1 tablespoon no-added-salt
  tomato sauce
2 teaspoons brown sugar
1 teaspoon cornflour
1 teaspoon water

Heat oil and garlic in pan, add mushrooms, cook for 2 minutes. Add shallots, pepper and cabbage, cook, covered, until cabbage is wilted. Stir in blended water, sauce, stock cube and cornflour. Divide mixture between wrappers, fold sides in, roll up.

Brush rolls lightly with egg white, place on baking paper-covered oven tray, bake in moderately hot oven for about 25 minutes or until lightly browned. Serve with sauce.
Sweet and Sour Sauce: Combine juice, vinegar, sauce and sugar in pan; blend cornflour and water, add to pan, stir over heat until sauce boils and thickens slightly.

Makes 6.

■ Not suitable to freeze.
■ Not suitable to microwave.
□ Total fat: 4.5g.
■ Fat per roll: Negligible.

LEFT: Vegetarian Spring Rolls with Sweet and Sour Sauce.

♥ ♥ ♥
CHILLI PIZZA ROUNDS

Make recipe just before serving.

2 tablespoons chopped fresh chives
60g low-fat cottage cheese
2 teaspoons chilli sauce
1 tablespoon honey
1 tablespoon no-added-salt
** tomato paste**
6 slices wholemeal bread
1 tablespoon grated parmesan
** cheese**

Combine chives, cheese, sauce, honey and paste in bowl. Cut 5cm rounds from bread, place rounds on oven trays, toast in moderate oven for about 10 minutes.

Spread rounds with prepared cheese mixture, sprinkle with parmesan. Bake in hot oven for about 10 minutes or until lightly browned.

Makes 6.
■ Not suitable to freeze.
■ Not suitable to microwave.
  Total fat: 7.4g.
■ Fat per pizza: 1.2g.

RIGHT: Chilli Pizza Rounds.

♥ ♥ ♥
BAGEL CHIPS

Traditionally, bagels do not contain fat or animal products; these are the correct ones to use for this recipe. Chips can be stored in an airtight container for a month.

2 bagels
2 teaspoons polyunsaturated oil
1 clove garlic, crushed
¼ teaspoon dried oregano leaves

Using a serrated or electric knife, cut bagels into very thin slices. Place slices in single layer on oven trays, very lightly brush 1 side of slices with combined oil, garlic and oregano. Bake in moderately slow oven for about 15 minutes or until lightly browned, cool chips on trays.
　　Serves 2.

■　Not suitable to freeze.
■　Not suitable to microwave.
□　Total fat: 9g.
■　Fat per serve: 4.5g.

♥ ♥ ♥
SALMON PARMESAN FINGERS

Make recipe just before serving.

2 slices wholemeal bread
105g can salmon, drained
½ small stick celery, finely chopped
2 teaspoons chopped fresh chives
4 drops tabasco sauce
1 tablespoon grated fresh parmesan cheese

Toast bread under hot grill until lightly browned on 1 side. Combine salmon, celery, chives and tabasco in bowl. Spread salmon mixture on untoasted side of bread, sprinkle with cheese. Grill until lightly browned.
　　Serves 2.

■　Not suitable to freeze.
■　Not suitable to microwave.
□　Total fat: 9g.
■　Fat per serve: 4.5g.

♥ ♥ ♥
FRUITY GINGER BALLS

Recipe can be made 2 days ahead.

¼ cup chopped dried apricots
¼ cup chopped dried apples
¼ cup chopped pitted prunes
2 teaspoons chopped glace ginger
2 tablespoons skim milk powder
1 tablespoon corn syrup
2 teaspoons brandy
10 flaked almonds, toasted

Combine fruit, ginger, skim milk powder, syrup and brandy in bowl. Roll rounded teaspoons of mixture into balls with slightly wet hands. Top each ball with a flaked almond.
　　Makes 10.

■　Not suitable to freeze.
□　Total fat: Negligible.

♥ ♥
MINI ASPARAGUS QUICHES

Make quiches just before serving.

PASTRY
⅓ cup wholemeal self-raising flour
⅓ cup plain flour
1 teaspoon grated lemon rind
2 teaspoons lemon juice
1 tablespoon corn syrup
1 egg white, lightly beaten
1 tablespoon water, approximately

FILLING
125g fresh asparagus, chopped
100g sachet Scramblers, lightly
    beaten
2 tablespoons grated reduced-fat
    tasty cheese
2 tablespoons buttermilk
1 tablespoon skim milk powder
1 tablespoon chopped fresh
    tarragon

Pastry: Sift flours into bowl, stir in combined rind, juice, syrup and egg white with enough water to make ingredients cling together (or process all ingredients until mixture forms a ball). Knead gently on lightly floured surface until smooth. Cover, refrigerate for 30 minutes. Roll pastry large enough to line 2 deep 9cm flan tins; trim edges.

Place asparagus into pastry cases, add filling. Place tins on oven tray, bake in hot oven for 10 minutes; reduce heat to moderate, bake for 25 minutes. Stand quiches for 5 minutes, then carefully remove from tins. Return quiches to oven tray, bake further 10 minutes or until pastry is cooked right through.

Filling: Boil, steam or microwave asparagus until soft; rinse under cold water, drain. Combine Scramblers and cheese in bowl, gradually stir in buttermilk, skim milk powder and tarragon.

Makes 2.

■ Not suitable to freeze.
■ Not suitable to microwave.
□ Total fat: 18.8g.
■ Fat per quiche: 9.4g.

LEFT: Clockwise from front: Salmon Parmesan Fingers, Fruity Ginger Balls, Bagel Chips.
BELOW: Mini Asparagus Quiches.

Sandwich
Fillings

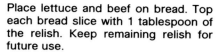

APRICOT RELISH OPEN SANDWICHES

Relish can be made 2 weeks ahead.

4 lettuce leaves
2 x 50g slices lean roast beef
2 slices dark rye bread
RELISH
⅔ cup chopped dried apricots
⅓ cup brown sugar
2 teaspoons yellow mustard seeds
1 onion, sliced
⅔ cup water
⅓ cup cider vinegar

Place lettuce and beef on bread. Top each bread slice with 1 tablespoon of the relish. Keep remaining relish for future use.
Relish: Combine all ingredients in pan, stir over heat until sugar is dissolved. Bring to boil, simmer for about 30 minutes or until thick, remove from heat, spoon into sterilised jar; seal when cold. You will have about 1 cup of relish.
     Makes 2.
■ Not suitable to freeze.
■ Not suitable to microwave.
    Total fat: 5.8g.
■ Fat per sandwich: 2.9g.

HERBED EGG SANDWICHES

Make sandwiches just before serving.

100g sachet Scramblers
2 teaspoons chopped fresh basil
1 tablespoon chopped fresh chives
1 tablespoon sour light cream
1 teaspoon seeded mustard
¼ cup alfalfa sprouts
4 slices rye bread

Combine Scramblers, herbs, cream and mustard in small pan, stir over low heat until mixture begins to set. Remove pan from heat, continue stirring until set. Spoon filling and sprouts onto 2 bread slices, top with remaining bread.
     Makes 2.
■ Not suitable to freeze.
■ Suitable to microwave.
    Total fat: 16.5g.
■ Fat per sandwich: 8.3g.

SPRING SALAD SANDWICHES

Filling can be made 3 hours ahead.

100g low-fat cottage cheese
8 English spinach leaves, chopped
1 green shallot, chopped
½ small carrot, grated
¼ cup mung bean sprouts
2 teaspoons sesame seeds, toasted
1 teaspoon lemon juice
4 slices wholemeal bread
¼ (50g) avocado

Combine cheese, spinach, shallot, carrot, sprouts, seeds and juice in bowl. Spread bread slices with avocado, top with filling; then top with remaining bread.
     Makes 2.
■ Not suitable to freeze.
    Total fat: 12g.
■ Fat per sandwich: 6g.

CURRIED TUNA SANDWICHES

Filling can be made a day ahead.

1 small tomato, sliced
4 slices rye bread
FILLING
½ x 185g can tuna in brine, drained, flaked
½ small stick celery, chopped
½ teaspoon curry powder
1 tablespoon chopped fresh parsley
1 tablespoon Light Coleslaw dressing

Divide tomato and filling between 2 bread slices; top with remaining bread.
Filling: Combine tuna, celery, curry powder and parsley in bowl, stir in dressing; mix well.
     Makes 2.
■ Not suitable to freeze.
    Total fat: 7g.
■ Fat per sandwich: 3.5g.

CHICKEN CELERY SANDWICHES

Make sandwiches just before serving.

4 slices wholemeal bread
SPREAD
200g chicken breast fillet
1 tablespoon lemon juice
¼ cup low-fat plain yogurt
¼ teaspoon hot English mustard
1 stick celery, chopped

Divide spread between 2 bread slices; top with remaining bread.
Spread: Poach, steam or microwave chicken until tender, cool; chop roughly.. Blend or process chicken, juice, yogurt and mustard until combined, stir in celery.
     Makes 2.
■ Not suitable to freeze.
    Total fat: 8g.
■ Fat per sandwich: 4g.

LEFT: Clockwise from front right: Chicken Celery Sandwiches, Herbed Egg Sandwiches, Apricot Relish Open Sandwiches, Curried Tuna Sandwiches, Spring Salad Sandwiches.

China from Villeroy & Boch; tiles from Northbridge Ceramic & Marble Centre

♥ ♥ ♥

SALMON AND CUCUMBER SANDWICHES

Filling can be made 3 hours ahead.

105g can pink salmon, drained
1 tablespoon low-fat cottage cheese
1 small green cucumber, chopped
2 teaspoons chopped fresh chives
4 slices wholemeal bread

Combine salmon, cheese, cucumber and chives in bowl. Spread mixture evenly over 2 bread slices, top with remaining bread.
Makes 2.
■ Not suitable to freeze.
■ Total fat: 9g.
□ Fat per sandwich: 3.5g.

♥ ♥ ♥

EGGPLANT TAHINI SANDWICHES

Filling can be made 3 days ahead.

4 slices wholemeal bread
1 cup shredded lettuce
1 tablespoon chopped fresh mint
FILLING
1 eggplant
1 tablespoon tahini paste
1 clove garlic, crushed
1½ tablespoons lemon juice

Spread 2 bread slices each with 2 tablespoons of the filling. Top with lettuce and mint, then remaining bread. Keep remaining filling for future use.
Filling: Halve eggplant, place on oven tray, bake in moderately hot oven for about 25 minutes or until soft, cool; remove skin. Blend or process eggplant, tahini, garlic and juice until well combined. You will have about 1 cup filling.
Makes 2.
■ Not suitable to freeze.
■ Not suitable to microwave.
□ Total fat: 13.4g.
■ Fat per sandwich: 3.3g.

♥ ♥ ♥

FRUITY RICOTTA SANDWICHES

Spread can be made a week ahead.

2 tablespoons low-fat ricotta cheese
4 slices wholemeal bread
SPREAD
⅓ cup chopped dried apricots
2 tablespoons chopped dried apples
1 cup orange juice
1¼ cups water

Divide cheese between 2 bread slices, top each slice with 1 tablespoon of spread; then remaining bread. Keep remaining spread for future use.
Spread: Combine all ingredients in pan, stir over heat until mixture boils, simmer, uncovered, for about 20 minutes or until mixture thickens, stir occasionally; cool. Blend or process mixture until smooth, spoon into sterilised jars, seal when cold. You will have about 1 cup spread.
■ Not suitable to freeze.
■ Suitable to microwave.
□ Total fat: 5.8g.
■ Fat per sandwich: 2.9g.

♥ ♥

COUSCOUS TABBOULEH POCKETS

Tabbouleh can be made a day ahead

1½ tablespoons couscous
¼ cup boiling water
½ cup chopped fresh parsley
1 small tomato, chopped
¼ small onion, chopped
1 tablespoon lemon juice
1 teaspoon chopped fresh mint
2 wholemeal pocket breads, halved
¼ (50g) avocado

Combine couscous and boiling water in bowl, stand 20 minutes or until water is absorbed; cool. Combine couscous, parsley, tomato, onion, juice and mint in bowl. Spread inside of breads with avocado, fill with tabbouleh.
Serves 2.
■ Not suitable to freeze.
□ Total fat: 12.4g.
■ Fat per serve: 6.2g.

ABOVE LEFT: From top: Couscous Tabbouleh Pockets, Salmon and Cucumber Sandwiches, Fruity Ricotta Sandwiches.
ABOVE RIGHT: Clockwise from back left: Pizza Pockets Filling, Eggplant Tahini Filling, Waldorf and Alfalfa Filling, Pumpkin Coleslaw Filling.

Above right: Bowls from Villa Italiana; table, bread boards and knife from Appley Hoare Antiques

♥ ♥ ♥
PIZZA POCKETS

Make filling close to serving time.

1 tomato, chopped
1 onion, chopped
100g button mushrooms, sliced
½ cup canned crushed pineapple,
 drained
½ red pepper, chopped
1 clove garlic, crushed
1 teaspoon dried oregano leaves
2 tablespoons grated fresh
 parmesan cheese
2 wholemeal pocket breads, halved

Combine tomato, onion, mushrooms,
pineapple and pepper in non-stick pan,
cook for about 5 minutes or until vegetables are soft. Stir in garlic, oregano
and cheese; cool. Spoon mixture into
pocket breads.
 Serves 2.
■ Not suitable to freeze.
■ Suitable to microwave.
□ Total fat: 9g.
■ Fat per serve: 4.5g.

♥ ♥ ♥
PUMPKIN COLESLAW
SANDWICHES

Make recipe just before serving.

4 slices wholemeal bread
COLESLAW
350g golden nugget pumpkin, grated
½ small red pepper, chopped
1 cup sliced cabbage
2 zucchini, grated
¼ cup light mayonnaise
¼ teaspoon dry mustard

Divide coleslaw between 2 bread
slices; top with remaining bread.
Coleslaw: Combine pumpkin, pepper,
cabbage and zucchini in bowl.
Combine mayonnaise and mustard in
bowl, stir into coleslaw.
 Makes 2.
■ Not suitable to freeze.
□ Total fat: 9.8g.
■ Fat per sandwich: 4.9g.

♥ ♥
WALDORF AND ALFALFA
SANDWICHES

Make filling just before serving.

4 slices wholemeal bread
½ cup alfalfa sprouts
WALDORF FILLING
1 stick celery, finely chopped
½ red apple, grated
2 tablespoons sour light cream

Spread waldorf filling over 2 bread
slices, top with alfalfa sprouts, then
remaining bread.
Waldorf Filling: Combine all ingre-
dients in bowl, mix well.
 Makes 2.
■ Not suitable to freeze.
□ Total fat: 11.4g.
■ Fat per sandwich: 5.7g.

Seafood

♥ ♥

FISH WITH PAPRIKA AND PIMIENTO SAUCE

Fish is best cooked close to serving time. Sauce can be made a day ahead.

2 x 200g white fish fillets
½ x 390g can pimientos, drained
SAUCE
2 teaspoons olive oil
1 small onion, chopped
2 teaspoons paprika
¾ cup water
½ vegetable stock cube, crumbled
2 teaspoons lemon juice
1 teaspoon sugar

Poach, steam or microwave fish until tender. Cut half a pimiento into strips; reserve remaining pimientos for sauce. Place pimiento strips on fish; serve with sauce.
Sauce: Chop reserved pimientos. Heat oil in pan, add onion, cook until soft. Stir in paprika, cook for 30 seconds. Stir in pimientos with remaining ingredients, bring to boil, simmer, uncovered, for 3 minutes. Blend or process mixture until smooth.
　Serves 2.
■ Not suitable to freeze.
■ Suitable to microwave.
■ Total fat: 11.8g.
■ Fat per serve: 5.9g.

♥ ♥ ♥

FISH IN WINE GARLIC MARINADE

Recipe can be prepared a day ahead.

2 x 250g whole leather jacket fish
1 clove garlic, crushed
½ teaspoon grated lemon rind
2 tablespoons lemon juice
1 tablespoon dry white wine
1 teaspoon olive oil
2 teaspoons chopped fresh thyme
½ teaspoon grated fresh ginger
½ teaspoon sugar

Place fish in shallow dish, pour over combined remaining ingredients, turn fish to coat in marinade; refrigerate for several hours or overnight.
　Remove fish from marinade, wrap in foil, place in baking dish. Bake in moderate oven for about 20 minutes or until fish are tender.
　Serves 2.
■ Not suitable to freeze.
■ Suitable to microwave.
■ Total fat: 6.6g.
■ Fat per serve: 3.3g.

♥ ♥

FISH CUTLETS WITH HERB CRUMBLE

Make recipe just before serving.

2 x 250g white fish cutlets
¾ cup stale wholemeal breadcrumbs
2 tablespoons lemon juice
2 tablespoons chopped fresh parsley
1 tablespoon chopped fresh chives
1 clove garlic, crushed

Cook fish under hot grill for 5 minutes, turn, sprinkle with combined breadcrumbs, juice, herbs and garlic, cook for about 5 minutes or until cooked through and lightly browned.
　Serves 2.
■ Not suitable to freeze.
■ Not suitable to microwave.
■ Total fat: 10.4g.
■ Fat per serve: 5.2g.

LEFT: Clockwise from back: Fish in Wine Garlic Marinade, Fish Cutlets with Herb Crumble, Fish with Paprika and Pimiento Sauce.

Dishes from Accoutrement

♥ ♥
TROPICAL FISH PATTIES

Recipe can be prepared a day ahead.

500g white fish fillets
¾ cup canned crushed pineapple,
**   drained**
½ small red pepper, chopped
½ small green pepper, chopped
1 tablespoon chopped fresh chives
100g pouch Just White Egg
**   White Mix**
1 cup stale breadcrumbs
¼ cup low-fat plain yogurt

Blend or process fish until smooth, combine with pineapple, peppers, chives, egg white mix, breadcrumbs and yogurt. Shape mixture into 8 patties, cook in heated non-stick pan until well browned on both sides and cooked through.
   Makes 8.
▫ Not suitable to freeze.
▪ Not suitable to microwave.
▫ Total fat: 11.6g.
▪ Fat per serve: 5.8g.

♥ ♥
FISH CUTLETS WITH CORIANDER CHILLI SAUCE

Make recipe close to serving time.

2 x 200g white fish cutlets
1 small onion, sliced
½ cup water
¼ cup dry vermouth
3 teaspoons lime juice
3 teaspoons polyunsaturated
**   margarine**
1 small fresh red chilli, finely
**   chopped**
2 teaspoons plain flour
½ vegetable stock cube, crumbled
1 tablespoon chopped fresh
**   coriander**

Place fish in shallow ovenproof dish, top with onion. Pour over combined water, vermouth and juice, cover, bake in moderate oven for about 20 minutes or until fish is tender. Remove fish; keep warm. Strain and reserve liquid.
   Heat margarine in pan, add chilli, cook for 30 seconds, stir in flour, cook until bubbling. Remove from heat, gradually stir in reserved liquid and stock cube, stir over heat until mixture boils and thickens; stir in coriander. Serve sauce over fish.
   Serves 2.
▫ Not suitable to freeze.
▪ Suitable to microwave.
▫ Total fat: 18.7g.
▪ Fat per serve: 9.4g.

♥ ♥
FISH TWISTS WITH BASIL AND PINE NUT DRESSING

Make recipe close to serving time.

2 x 150g whiting fillets
1 tomato
1 eggplant
DRESSING
⅓ cup red wine vinegar
2 tablespoons honey
2 tablespoons chopped fresh basil
1 clove garlic, crushed
1 tablespoon pine nuts, toasted

Cut each fillet lengthways into 3 strips. Cut tomato and eggplant into 6 slices each. Top eggplant slices with tomato and fish strips. Steam over simmering water for about 5 minutes or until fish is tender. Serve with dressing.
Dressing: Combine all ingredients in bowl; mix well.
   Serves 2.
▫ Not suitable to freeze.
▪ Suitable to microwave.
▫ Total fat: 11.5g.
▪ Fat per serve: 5.6g.

ABOVE: Fish Twists with Basil and Pine Nut Dressing.
RIGHT: Clockwise from top: Chilli Seafood Rice, Tropical Fish Patties, Fish Cutlets with Coriander Chilli Sauce.

Above: Plate from Casa Shopping, fork from The Bay Tree. Right: Plates from The Australian East India Co.

♥ ♥
CHILLI SEAFOOD RICE

Recipe can be made a day ahead.

2 teaspoons polyunsaturated oil
1 small onion, chopped
1 clove garlic, crushed
410g can no-added-salt tomatoes
1 small fresh red chilli, finely
**   chopped**
¼ cup dry red wine
430g can chicken consomme
½ cup long grain rice
1 tablespoon chopped fresh parsley
1 small red pepper, chopped
1 small green pepper, chopped
375g white fish fillets, chopped
100g crab meat
125g scallops

Heat oil in pan, add onion and garlic, cook until soft. Add tomatoes, chilli, wine and consomme, bring to boil, gradually stir in rice, simmer, uncovered, for about 15 minutes or until rice is just tender. Add parsley, peppers and seafood, gently stir over heat for about 5 minutes or until peppers are soft and seafood tender.
   Serves 2.
▫ Not suitable to freeze.
▪ Not suitable to microwave.
▫ Total fat: 13.5g.
▪ Fat per serve: 6.8g.

SPINACH AND PUMPKIN RING WITH SCALLOP SAUCE

Make recipe close to serving time.

½ bunch (20 leaves) English spinach
FILLING
**1 teaspoon polyunsaturated
    margarine
5 green shallots, sliced
400g butternut pumpkin, chopped
½ cup water
⅔ cup buttermilk
¼ cup skim milk powder
¼ teaspoon ground nutmeg
2 egg whites**
SCALLOP SAUCE
**1 teaspoon polyunsaturated
    margarine
5 green shallots, sliced
1 tablespoon water
1 tablespoon plain flour
1 cup skim milk
1 teaspoon no-added-salt
    tomato paste
100g scallops**

Trim spinach leaves, place spinach in pan of boiling water until just wilted; drain on absorbent paper. Lightly grease 20cm savarin ring pan. Line pan with spinach, allowing spinach to overhang edge of pan, spoon in filling, fold spinach over to enclose filling.

Cover pan with lightly greased foil, place in baking dish with enough hot water to come half way up side of pan. Bake in moderately hot oven for about 45 minutes or until mixture is puffed slightly and set. Stand for 5 minutes before turning out. Serve ring with warm scallop sauce.

Filling: Heat margarine in pan, add shallots and pumpkin, cook until shallots are soft. Add water, bring to boil, simmer, covered, for about 15 minutes or until pumpkin is soft; cool slightly. Blend or process pumpkin mixture with buttermilk, skim milk powder and nutmeg until smooth; transfer mixture to bowl. Beat egg whites until soft peaks form, gently fold into pumpkin mixture.

Scallop Sauce: Heat margarine in pan, add shallots and water, cook until soft, stir in flour, cook for 1 minute. Remove from heat, gradually stir in milk and paste, stir over heat until mixture boils and thickens. Separate roe from scallops; push roe through fine strainer; thinly slice white part of scallops. Combine roe and white part of scallops with sauce mixture.

Serves 2.
■ Not suitable to freeze.
■ Not suitable to microwave.
□ Total fat: 13.8g.
■ Fat per serve: 6.9g.

HEARTY OYSTER SOUP

Make recipe close to serving time.

**2 teaspoons polyunsaturated
    margarine
1 small onion, chopped
1 clove garlic, crushed
1¼ cups water
1 cup skim milk
½ vegetable stock cube,
    crumbled
2 potatoes, chopped
2 tablespoons no-added-salt
    tomato paste
¼ teaspoon cracked black
    peppercorns
12 oysters
1 tablespoon chopped fresh chives
1 tablespoon sour light cream**

Heat margarine in pan, add onion and garlic, cook until soft. Add water, milk, stock cube, potatoes, paste and peppercorns, bring to boil, simmer, covered, for about 8 minutes or until potato is soft; cool slightly.

Blend or process undrained mixture until smooth, return to pan, add oysters and chives, stir over heat until soup is heated through. Serve topped with cream.

Serves 2.
■ Not suitable to freeze.
■ Not suitable to microwave.
□ Total fat: 15.8g.
■ Fat per serve: 7.9g.

SALMON AND HERB SOUFFLES

Cook recipe just before serving.

**210g can salmon, drained
1 tablespoon chopped fresh chives
1 tablespoon chopped fresh parsley
pinch cayenne pepper
1 tablespoon polyunsaturated
    margarine
1 tablespoon plain flour
½ cup skim milk
2 egg whites**

Grease 2 souffle dishes (1 cup capacity). Combine salmon, herbs and pepper in bowl; mix well. Heat margarine in pan, stir in flour; cook until bubbling. Remove from heat, gradually stir in milk, stir over heat until sauce boils and thickens.

Stir sauce into salmon mixture. Beat egg whites until soft peaks form, fold into salmon mixture. Spoon mixture into prepared dishes, bake in moderate oven for about 20 minutes or until risen and well browned.

Serves 2.
■ Not suitable to freeze.
■ Not suitable to microwave.
□ Total fat: 27g.
■ Fat per serve: 13.5g.

ABOVE: Spinach and Pumpkin Ring with Scallop Sauce.

♥ ♥ ♥

FISH QUENELLES WITH APPLE CELERY SAUCE

Quenelle mixture is best made just before serving. Sauce can be made a day ahead.

1 cup dry white wine
½ cup water
1 bay leaf
1 onion, quartered
QUENELLES
250g redfish fillets
2 egg whites
2 tablespoons low-fat plain yogurt
1 tablespoon lemon juice

APPLE CELERY SAUCE
1 stick celery, chopped
1 onion, chopped
1 apple, chopped
1 tablespoon lemon juice
¾ cup water
1 green shallot, chopped
1 tablespoon chopped fresh chives

Combine wine, water, bay leaf and onion in pan, bring to boil, simmer, uncovered, for 5 minutes, strain; discard onion and bay leaf. Return liquid to pan, simmer.

Mould quenelle mixture into oval shapes using 2 wet teaspoons. Spoon ovals into simmering liquid, poach for about 1 minute on each side. Do not allow water to come to the boil or quenelles will fall apart. Drain quenelles on absorbent paper, serve with sauce.

Quenelles: Blend or process fish, egg whites, yogurt and juice until smooth.
Apple Celery Sauce: Combine celery, onion, apple, juice and water in pan, bring to boil, simmer, covered, for about 10 minutes or until vegetables are soft. Stir in shallot; cool slightly. Blend or process mixture until smooth; stir in chives.

Serves 2.
◼ Not suitable to freeze.
◼ Not suitable to microwave.
◻ Total fat: 4.5g.
◼ Fat per serve: 2.3g.

BELOW: Clockwise from front: Salmon and Herb Souffles, Fish Quenelles with Apple Celery Sauce, Hearty Oyster Soup.

Tiles from Northbridge Ceramic & Marble Centre

♥ ♥
HERBED MUSSELS AND FISH

Cook recipe just before serving.

12 large mussels
2 teaspoons olive oil
1 onion, sliced
1 clove garlic, crushed
1 stick celery, chopped
410g can no-added-salt tomatoes
1 tablespoon no-added-salt
tomato paste
¼ cup dry white wine
½ cup water
1 teaspoon chopped fresh thyme
300g white fish fillet, chopped
2 teaspoons chopped fresh parsley

Remove beards from mussels, scrub shells. Heat oil in pan, add onion and garlic, cover, cook until soft. Add celery, undrained crushed tomatoes, paste, wine, water and thyme. Bring to boil, boil for 2 minutes. Add mussels and fish, stir gently, simmer, covered, for about 5 minutes or until seafood is tender. Serve sprinkled with parsley.
Serves 2.
■ Not suitable to freeze.
■ Not suitable to microwave.
Total fat: 16.9g.
■ Fat per serve: 8.5g.

♥ ♥
FISH KEBABS
WITH CHILLI SAUCE

Recipe can be prepared a day ahead.

300g white fish fillets, chopped
1 tablespoon salt-reduced soy sauce
1 clove garlic, crushed
¼ teaspoon grated fresh ginger
1 red pepper, chopped
1 green pepper, chopped
2 teaspoons polyunsaturated oil
1 cup cooked rice

CHILLI SAUCE
1 small fresh red chilli, chopped
2 cloves garlic, crushed
1 tablespoon chopped fresh
coriander
1 tablespoon fish sauce
1 tablespoon lime juice
1½ tablespoons brown sugar
1 teaspoon polyunsaturated oil
2 teaspoons cornflour
1 tablespoon mirin
¾ cup water

Combine fish with sauce, garlic and ginger in bowl; refrigerate for 1 hour. Thread fish and peppers alternately onto 4 skewers. Brush with oil, cook under hot grill until fish is tender. Serve on rice with sauce.

Chilli Sauce: Grind chilli, garlic and coriander to a smooth paste. Add fish sauce, juice and sugar. Heat oil in pan, add chilli mixture, stir until sugar is dissolved; stir in blended cornflour and mirin with water, stir until sauce boils and thickens.
Serves 2.
■ Not suitable to freeze.
■ Suitable to microwave.
Total fat: 17.2g.
■ Fat per serve: 8.6g.

ABOVE: Herbed Mussels and Fish.
RIGHT: From top: Fish Kebabs with Chilli Sauce, Curried Fish Crumble, Rolled Fish Fillets with Mushroom Sauce.

Right: Serving ware from The Australian East India Co.

CURRIED FISH CRUMBLE

Recipe can be made 3 hours ahead.

350g mullet fillets
1 teaspoon polyunsaturated
   margarine
1 onion, chopped
1 bunch (40 leaves) English spinach,
   shredded
1 carrot, sliced
1 parsnip, sliced
1 tablespoon cornflour
1 cup skim milk
½ vegetable stock cube, crumbled
1 teaspoon curry powder
CRUMBLE TOPPING
¼ cup rolled oats
¼ cup grated parmesan cheese
2 tablespoons wholemeal plain flour
2 teaspoons polyunsaturated
   margarine
1 tablespoon chopped fresh chives

Place fish in pan, cover with water, bring to boil, simmer, uncovered, for about 3 minutes or until fish is tender. Drain, remove and discard skin; flake fish into bowl.

Heat margarine in pan, add onion, cook until soft. Add spinach, cook, stirring, until spinach is wilted. Spoon spinach mixture into 2 ovenproof dishes (2 cup capacity).

Boil, steam or microwave carrot and parsnip until tender, place on top of spinach, then top with fish.

Blend cornflour with milk in pan, stir in stock cube and curry powder. Stir over heat until sauce boils and thickens; pour over fish. Sprinkle topping over sauce, bake in moderate oven for about 30 minutes or until heated through and lightly browned.
Crumble Topping: Combine oats, cheese and flour in bowl, rub in margarine; stir in chives.
   Serves 2.
■ Not suitable to freeze.
■ Not suitable to microwave.
   Total fat: 24.7g.
■ Fat per serve: 12.4g.

ROLLED FISH FILLETS WITH MUSHROOM SAUCE

Make recipe close to serving time.

6 x 70g redfish fillets
2 teaspoons lemon juice
MUSHROOM SAUCE
2 teaspoons polyunsaturated
   margarine
2 teaspoons plain flour
¾ cup skim milk
¼ cup water
½ small chicken stock cube,
   crumbled
3 green shallots, chopped
60g small mushrooms, sliced
1 tablespoon dry white wine
1 teaspoon lemon juice
¼ teaspoon dried thyme leaves
2 teaspoons sour light cream

Roll fish fillets, secure with toothpicks, drizzle with lemon juice. Steam for about 5 minutes or until tender. Serve with sauce.
Mushroom Sauce: Heat margarine in pan, stir in flour, cook until bubbling. Remove from heat, gradually stir in combined milk, water and stock cube, shallots, mushrooms, wine, juice and thyme, stir over heat until mixture boils and thickens, stir in sour cream.
   Serves 2.
■ Not suitable to freeze.
■ Suitable to microwave.
   Total fat: 18.5g.
■ Fat per serve: 9.2g.

Poultry

♥ ♥ ♥
ROLLED TURKEY WITH NUTTY SPINACH SEASONING

Recipe can be made a day ahead.

400g turkey breast fillet
NUTTY SPINACH SEASONING
¼ cup cooked rice
1 spinach (silverbeet) leaf, chopped
2 green shallots, chopped
**1 tablespoon roasted chopped
    hazelnuts**
1 teaspoon grated lemon rind
1 teaspoon chopped fresh thyme
1 egg white
CRANBERRY SAUCE
2 tablespoons cranberry sauce
1 teaspoon brandy
½ teaspoon grated orange rind
2 tablespoons water

Remove skin from turkey, pound turkey until thin, spread evenly with seasoning, roll turkey from short end, secure with string.

Place turkey in oven bag, bake in moderate oven for about 40 minutes or until tender. Remove turkey from oven bag, cool; remove string. Cut into slices, serve cold with sauce.

Nutty Spinach Seasoning: Combine all ingredients in bowl.

Cranberry Sauce: Strain sauce into bowl, stir in remaining ingredients.

Serves 4.
■ Not suitable to freeze.
■ Suitable to microwave.
□ Total fat: 12.4g.
■ Fat per serve: 3.1g.

♥ ♥ ♥
MINTED TURKEY SLICE

Recipe is best made a day ahead.

2 small green cucumbers, sliced
2 teaspoons gelatine
1 tablespoon water
200g piece cooked turkey breast roll
½ red pepper, finely chopped
2 tablespoons chopped fresh mint
2 tablespoons dry sherry
425g can chicken consomme
1 tablespoon chopped fresh chives
1 tablespoon gelatine, extra
¼ cup water, extra

Arrange cucumber slices in 8cm x 26cm bar pan.

Sprinkle gelatine over water in cup, stand in small pan of simmering water, stir until dissolved; pour evenly over cucumbers. Refrigerate until set.

Chop turkey into 1cm cubes. Combine turkey, pepper, mint, sherry, consomme and chives in bowl.

Sprinkle extra gelatine over extra water in cup, stand in small pan of simmering water, stir until dissolved; cool slightly. Stir extra gelatine mixture into turkey mixture, pour mixture into pan; refrigerate until set.

Serves 2.
■ Not suitable to freeze.
■ Not suitable to microwave.
□ Total fat: 5.4g.
■ Fat per serve: 2.7g.

*RIGHT: From left: Minted Turkey Slice,
Rolled Turkey with Nutty Spinach
Seasoning.*

China, table and chair from The Country Trader

Blend or process chicken, cheese, cinnamon and parsley until mixture is almost smooth. Place a teaspoon of mixture onto centre of each wrapper, brush edges with water, gather edges together to form a pouch. Add dumplings to large pan of boiling water, simmer, uncovered, for about 8 minutes or until cooked through; drain. Serve with spinach and sultanas.

Spinach and Sultanas: Combine spinach, pepper and carrot in non-stick pan, cook, covered, until pepper is soft. Stir in sultanas, juice, almonds and buttermilk, stir until hot.

Serves 2.
- Not suitable to freeze.
- Suitable to microwave.
- Total fat: 22g.
- Fat per serve: 11g.

♥
POLENTA DRUMSTICKS WITH CURRY SAUCE

Make recipe just before serving.

4 chicken drumsticks
100g pouch Just White Egg White Mix
1 cup polenta
½ cup skim milk
1 onion, finely chopped
1 teaspoon ground cumin
½ teaspoon ground coriander
1 teaspoon garam masala
½ teaspoon ground black pepper
1 teaspoon sugar
1 clove garlic, crushed
1 small fresh red chilli, chopped
1 tablespoon cornflour
1 tablespoon skim milk, extra

Remove skin from drumsticks, dip drumsticks into egg white mix, roll in polenta, place onto non-stick oven tray. Bake in moderate oven for about 45 minutes or until chicken is tender.

Combine milk, onion, spices, sugar, garlic and chilli in pan, bring to boil, boil for 1 minute. Stir in blended cornflour and extra milk, stir until sauce boils and thickens. Blend or process sauce until smooth. Serve with drumsticks.

Serves 2.
- Not suitable to freeze.
- Not suitable to microwave.
- Total fat: 25.3g.
- Fat per serve: 12.7g.

ABOVE: Chicken and Artichoke Pies.
RIGHT: From top: Polenta Drumsticks with Curry Sauce, Chicken Dumplings with Spinach and Sultanas.

Right: Tiles from Northbridge Ceramic & Marble Centre

♥ ♥ ♥
CHICKEN AND ARTICHOKE PIES

Make recipe just before serving.

1 tablespoon dry white wine
½ cup water
1 stick celery, chopped
2 teaspoons chopped fresh oregano
1 onion, chopped
½ small chicken stock cube, crumbled
1 tablespoon plain flour
½ cup skim milk
375g chicken breast fillets, chopped
390g can artichokes in brine, drained, chopped
2 sheets fillo pastry

Combine wine, water, celery, oregano, onion and stock cube in pan, bring to boil, simmer, uncovered, until onion is soft. Stir in blended flour and milk, stir until mixture boils and thickens. Stir in chicken and artichokes, simmer, uncovered, for about 5 minutes or until chicken is tender.

Spoon mixture into 2 ovenproof dishes (1½ cup capacity).

Cut 1 pastry sheet lengthways into quarters, cut remaining sheet crossways into 8. Roll strips of pastry, gathering on 1 edge, to form roses, trim, arrange roses on top of each pie.

Place pies on oven tray, bake in moderately hot oven for about 15 minutes or until pastry is lightly browned and crisp.

Serves 2.
- Not suitable to freeze.
- Not suitable to microwave.
- Total fat: 8.6g.
- Fat per serve: 4.3g.

♥
CHICKEN DUMPLINGS WITH SPINACH AND SULTANAS

Dumplings can be made a day ahead.

200g chicken thigh fillets, chopped
50g reduced-fat feta cheese, mashed
¼ teaspoon ground cinnamon
2 tablespoons chopped fresh parsley
100g packet round gow gee wrappers
SPINACH AND SULTANAS
½ bunch (20 leaves) English spinach, shredded
1 red pepper, sliced
1 carrot, chopped
¼ cup sultanas
1 tablespoon lemon juice
1 tablespoon flaked almonds
⅓ cup buttermilk

♥ ♥
GRILLED TANDOORI CHICKEN

Recipe can be prepared a day ahead.

½ cup low-fat plain yogurt
1 tablespoon lemon juice
½ teaspoon grated fresh ginger
1 clove garlic, crushed
½ teaspoon castor sugar
½ teaspoon paprika
¼ teaspoon ground cumin
¼ teaspoon ground coriander
¼ teaspoon turmeric
pinch chilli powder
2 x 200g chicken breast fillets

Combine yogurt, juice, ginger, garlic, sugar, paprika and spices in bowl. Add chicken, turn chicken to coat in marinade; refrigerate for several hours or overnight. Grill chicken, brushing with marinade, until browned on both sides and tender.

Serves 2.
■ Not suitable to freeze.
■ Not suitable to microwave.
□ Total fat: 9.2g.
■ Fat per serve: 4.6g.

♥ ♥ ♥
SMOKED CHICKEN WITH SHERRY SAUCE

Sauce can be made 2 days ahead. Cook chicken just before serving.

½ cup Chinese assorted spices
¼ cup sugar
2 tablespoons black peppercorns
¼ cup uncooked rice
2 x 150g chicken breast fillets
1 cup cooked rice

SHERRY SAUCE
¼ cup dry sherry
¼ cup water
1 teaspoon sugar
1 teaspoon chopped fresh ginger
1½ teaspoons cornflour
1½ tablespoons salt-reduced
    soy sauce
1 green shallot, sliced

Line wok with foil. Combine spices, sugar, peppercorns and uncooked rice in wok. Place a rack in wok above spice mixture. Place chicken on rack, cover wok with tight lid, cook over medium heat for about 25 minutes or until chicken is tender. Serve chicken with sauce and cooked rice.

Sherry Sauce: Combine sherry, water, sugar and ginger in pan, stir in blended cornflour and sauce. Stir over heat until mixture boils and thickens, stir in shallot, mix well.

Serves 2.
■ Not suitable to freeze.
■ Not suitable to microwave.
□ Total fat: 7g.
■ Fat per serve: 3.5g.

♥ CHICKEN LOAF WITH TOMATO CHILLI SAUCE

Loaf can be made several hours ahead. Sauce can be made a day ahead.

200g chicken breast fillets, chopped
2 teaspoons olive oil
¼ small leek, sliced
½ small red pepper, sliced
2 teaspoons plain flour
⅓ cup skim milk
¼ cup stale white breadcrumbs
1 tablespoon grated parmesan cheese
1 egg white, lightly beaten
1 tablespoon chopped fresh tarragon

TOMATO CHILLI SAUCE
1 teaspoon olive oil
½ small onion, chopped
1 small tomato, peeled, chopped
1 small fresh red chilli, chopped
1 teaspoon no-added-salt tomato paste
1 teaspoon lemon juice

Lightly grease 2 small loaf pans (¾ cup capacity), line base with paper, lightly grease paper.

Blend or process chicken until finely chopped. Heat oil in pan, add leek and pepper, cook until leek is soft, stir in flour, cook for 1 minute. Gradually stir in milk, stir over heat until mixture boils and thickens.

Combine leek mixture with chicken and remaining ingredients in bowl. Spoon mixture into prepared pans, place pans in baking dish with enough boiling water to come halfway up sides of pans. Bake in moderate oven for about 25 minutes or until firm. Stand in pans for 5 minutes before turning onto wire rack to cool. Serve with tomato chilli sauce.

Tomato Chilli Sauce: Heat oil in pan, add onion, cook until soft. Stir in remaining ingredients, simmer, uncovered, for 2 minutes; cool.

Serves 2.
- ■ Not suitable to freeze.
- ■ Not suitable to microwave.
- ▢ Total fat: 21.3g.
- ■ Fat per serve: 10.6g.

ABOVE LEFT: From top: Grilled Tandoori Chicken, Smoked Chicken with Sherry Sauce.
ABOVE RIGHT: From top: Chicken Loaf with Tomato Chilli Sauce, Brandied Turkey Pate.

Above left: Plates from Accoutrement; plant from Liquidamber Nursery. Above right: China from Shop 3, Balmain; table from Corso de Fiori

♥ ♥ ♥ BRANDIED TURKEY PATE

Pate can be made 2 days ahead.

1 wholemeal pita bread
200g turkey breast fillet, chopped
1 onion, chopped
1 eggplant, chopped
1 tablespoon wholemeal plain flour
1 tablespoon chopped fresh basil
½ cup water
2 tablespoons brandy
1 tablespoon canned drained green peppercorns
2 teaspoons gelatine
¼ cup water, extra

Cut bread into 8 wedges, place on oven tray, bake in moderate oven for about 15 minutes or until crisp.

Combine turkey, onion and eggplant in non-stick pan, stir over heat until well browned. Stir in flour, cook for 3 minutes. Stir in basil and water, bring to boil; cool.

Blend or process turkey mixture and brandy until almost smooth. Stir in peppercorns. Spoon mixture into mould (2 cup capacity). Sprinkle gelatine over extra water in cup, stand in small pan of simmering water, stir until dissolved. Pour over pate, decorate with herbs, if desired; refrigerate until set. Serve pate with bread wedges.

Serves 2.
- ▢ Not suitable to freeze.
- ■ Suitable to microwave.
- ▢ Total fat: 5.8g.
- ■ Fat per serve: 2.9g.

♥ GRILLED QUAIL WITH REDCURRANT SAUCE

Cook quail just before serving.

4 quail
2 cups dry white wine
¼ cup white wine vinegar
4 black peppercorns
1 clove
1 bay leaf
1 small carrot, chopped
½ stick celery, chopped
1 small onion, chopped
2 parsley sprigs, chopped
1 teaspoon polyunsaturated oil
REDCURRANT SAUCE
2 tablespoons redcurrant jelly
1 teaspoon cornflour
3 teaspoons water
2 tablespoons fresh or frozen
   redcurrants

Using scissors, cut down both sides of backbone of each quail. Remove and discard backbones. Using heel of hand, press quail flat. Trim wings to second joint, remove skin and any visible fat from quail. Place quail in single layer in shallow dish.

Combine wine, vinegar, peppercorns, clove, bay leaf, carrot, celery, onion and parsley in bowl; pour over quail; refrigerate for 2 hours. Remove quail from marinade; reserve marinade. Pat quail dry with absorbent paper, brush with oil, grill until lightly browned and tender. Serve with sauce.

Redcurrant Sauce: Place reserved marinade in pan, bring to boil, simmer, uncovered, for 3 minutes. Remove from heat, strain; return 1 cup of liquid to pan. Bring to boil; boil until reduced by half. Add jelly, stir until dissolved. Stir in blended cornflour and water, stir until mixture boils and thickens; stir in redcurrants.

Serves 2.
■ Not suitable to freeze.
■ Not suitable to microwave.
□ Total fat: 22g.
■ Fat per serve: 11g.

♥ ♥ GINGER CHICKEN KEBABS

Cook recipe just before serving.

300g chicken breast fillets, chopped
1 tablespoon green ginger wine
1 tablespoon salt-reduced soy sauce
1 tablespoon lemon juice
1 teaspoon polyunsaturated oil
2 teaspoons Worcestershire sauce
2 teaspoons brown sugar
½ teaspoon dry mustard
1 teaspoon grated fresh ginger

Combine chicken and remaining ingredients in bowl, refrigerate for several hours. Thread chicken onto skewers, reserve marinade. Grill kebabs, brushing with marinade, until chicken is tender.

Serves 2.
■ Not suitable to freeze.
■ Suitable to microwave.
□ Total fat: 11.4g.
■ Fat per serve: 5.7g.

♥ ♥ ♥ FRUITY CHICKEN CURRY

Recipe can be made a day ahead.

1 teaspoon polyunsaturated oil
1 onion, chopped
1 teaspoon ground cumin
1 teaspoon curry powder
410g can no-added-salt tomatoes
¼ cup chutney
2 tablespoons honey
1 tablespoon white vinegar
200g chicken breast fillets, chopped
2 bananas, chopped

Heat oil in pan, add onion, cumin, curry powder and juice from tomatoes, cook until onion is soft. Add crushed tomatoes, chutney, honey and vinegar, bring to boil, simmer, uncovered, for about 5 minutes or until mixture is thick. Stir in chicken and bananas, simmer for about 5 minutes or until chicken is tender.

Serves 2.
■ Not suitable to freeze.
■ Suitable to microwave.
□ Total fat: 9g.
■ Fat per serve: 4.5g.

LEFT: Clockwise from front: Ginger Chicken Kebabs, Fruity Chicken Curry, Grilled Quail with Redcurrant Sauce.

Serving ware from Villa Italiana; cutlery and table from Appley Hoare Antiques

Rabbit

RABBIT AND TOMATO VEGETABLE CASSEROLE

Make casserole just before serving.

450g rabbit pieces
½ cup fresh or frozen peas
200g pumpkin, chopped
½ red pepper, chopped
1 large onion, chopped
415ml can tomato puree
1 clove garlic, crushed
½ cup dry white wine
2 tablespoons chopped fresh parsley
½ cup water

Combine all ingredients in pan, bring to boil, simmer, covered, for about 1¼ hours or until rabbit is tender.
   Serves 2.
■ Suitable to freeze.
■ Suitable to microwave.
■ Total fat: 9.2g.
■ Fat per serve: 4.6g.

SWEET AND SOUR BAKED RABBIT

Make recipe just before serving.

1 teaspoon olive oil
450g rabbit pieces
2 tablespoons no-added-salt tomato sauce
1 tablespoon cider vinegar
½ teaspoon sugar
1 tablespoon plain flour
1 small green pepper, chopped
225g can pineapple pieces
1 tablespoon chopped fresh parsley

Heat oil in non-stick pan, add rabbit, cook until browned all over. Drain rabbit on absorbent paper; place in oven bag.
   Combine sauce, vinegar, sugar and flour in bowl; stir in remaining ingredients. Pour mixture over rabbit in bag, seal bag, pierce bag several times near sealed end, place bag in baking dish, bake in moderate oven for about 1¼ hours or until rabbit is tender.
   Serves 2.
■ Not suitable to freeze.
■ Not suitable to microwave.
■ Total fat: 13.7g.
■ Fat per serve: 6.9g.

ABOVE: Rabbit and Tomato Vegetable Casserole.
RIGHT: From top: Sweet and Sour Baked Rabbit, Hearty Rabbit Stew.

Above: Dish from Barbara's House and Garden

♥ ♥

HEARTY RABBIT STEW

Cook recipe close to serving time.

400g rabbit pieces
1 tablespoon plain flour
1 teaspoon olive oil
¾ cup water
½ cup dry white wine
2 teaspoons no-added-salt tomato paste
½ small chicken stock cube, crumbled
1 carrot, chopped
1 potato, chopped
4 baby onions
½ cup frozen peas

Toss rabbit in flour, shake away excess flour. Heat oil in pan, add rabbit, cook until rabbit is browned all over. Stir in water, wine, paste and stock cube, bring to boil, simmer, covered, for 1 hour. Add carrot, potato and onions, cook for 15 minutes, add peas, cook until vegetables are tender.

Serves 2.

■ Not suitable to freeze.
■ Not suitable to microwave.
□ Total fat: 12.5g.
■ Fat per serve: 6.3g.

Vegetarian

♥ ♥ ♥
HERBED RATATOUILLE WITH PASTA

Sauce can be made a day ahead.

1 teaspoon olive oil
1 clove garlic, crushed
1 onion, chopped
1 eggplant, chopped
4 zucchini, chopped
1 green pepper, chopped
2 tomatoes, chopped
1 tablespoon dry red wine
1 tablespoon no-added-salt tomato paste
1 tablespoon chopped fresh basil
300g pasta

Heat oil in non-stick pan, add garlic and onion, cook until soft. Stir in eggplant, cook until eggplant is soft, remove from pan; drain on absorbent paper. Cook zucchini and pepper separately, following same method as eggplant. Return vegetables with tomatoes, wine, paste and basil to pan, cook for 5 minutes or until mixture is heated through.

Add pasta to large pan of boiling water, boil, uncovered, until just tender; drain. Serve with ratatouille.

Serves 2.
■ Not suitable to freeze.
■ Suitable to microwave.
□ Total fat: 8.4g.
■ Fat per serve: 4.2g.

♥ ♥
SPINACH MARJORAM CREPES

Crepes can be made 2 days ahead. Sauce can be made a day ahead. Assemble crepes just before serving.

1 bunch (40 leaves) English spinach
125g reduced-fat ricotta cheese
2 tablespoons grated parmesan cheese
1 teaspoon chopped fresh marjoram

CREPES
¼ cup plain flour
1 egg white
⅓ cup skim milk
SAUCE
½ cup skim milk
2 teaspoons no-added-salt tomato paste
¼ small chicken stock cube, crumbled
1 bay leaf
1 teaspoon plain flour
1 teaspoon polyunsaturated margarine

Boil, steam or microwave spinach until tender; drain on absorbent paper, cool; chop roughly.

Combine spinach, cheeses and marjoram in bowl. Spread crepes with spinach mixture, roll crepes, place in ovenproof dish. Cover, bake in moderate oven for about 20 minutes or until heated through. Serve crepes with sauce.

Crepes: Sift flour into bowl, gradually stir in combined egg white and milk to make a smooth batter.

Pour quarter of the batter into heated non-stick crepe pan, cook until lightly browned underneath. Turn crepe, brown on other side. Repeat with remaining batter.

Sauce: Combine milk, paste, stock cube and bay leaf in pan, bring to boil, stir in combined flour and margarine. Stir until sauce boils and thickens; strain, discard bay leaf.

Serves 2.
■ Not suitable to freeze.
■ Not suitable to microwave.
□ Total fat: 16.9g.
■ Fat per serve: 8.5g.

LEFT: Clockwise from front: Spinach Marjoram Crepes, Herbed Ratatouille with Pasta, Vegetarian Pizza.

China from Villa Italiana; plant from Liquidamber Nursery;

♥ ♥
VEGETARIAN PIZZA

Pizza can be prepared 3 hours ahead.

15g compressed yeast
½ teaspoon sugar
½ cup water
1½ cups plain flour
1 teaspoon polyunsaturated oil
¼ cup no-added-salt tomato paste
½ cup canned drained kidney beans
1 small onion, sliced
1 small zucchini, sliced
1 small red pepper, sliced
4 baby mushrooms, sliced
¾ cup bean sprouts
¼ teaspoon dried basil leaves
¼ teaspoon dried oregano leaves
¼ cup grated light mozzarella cheese
1 tablespoon grated parmesan cheese

Cream yeast with sugar in bowl, stir in water. Cover, stand in warm place for about 10 minutes or until mixture is frothy. Sift flour into bowl, stir in yeast mixture and oil, mix to a firm dough.

Turn dough onto floured surface, knead for about 5 minutes or until dough is smooth and elastic.

Return dough to bowl, cover, stand in warm place for about 45 minutes or until doubled in size. Turn dough onto lightly floured surface, knead until smooth.

Roll dough large enough to line 20cm pizza tray. Spread dough with paste, top with remaining ingredients. Bake in moderately hot oven for about 25 minutes or until crust is crisp.

Serves 2.
■ Suitable to freeze.
■ Not suitable to microwave.
□ Total fat: 15.1g.
■ Fat per serve: 7.6g.

VEGETABLE RISOTTO

Risotto can be made 3 hours ahead.

1 small eggplant, chopped
salt
2 teaspoons olive oil
1 small onion, chopped
1 clove garlic, crushed
¾ cup brown rice
½ small chicken stock cube,
    crumbled
2¾ cups water
1 small red pepper, chopped
2 tomatoes, peeled, chopped
2 zucchini, thinly sliced
125g mushrooms, sliced
2 teaspoons chopped fresh oregano
¼ cup grated parmesan cheese

Place eggplant in colander, sprinkle with salt, stand for 30 minutes. Rinse well under cold water, pat dry with absorbent paper.

Heat oil in pan, add onion and garlic, cook until soft. Add rice, stock cube and water, bring to boil, simmer, covered, for about 30 minutes or until rice is tender and almost all the liquid is absorbed.

Stir in eggplant, pepper, tomatoes, zucchini, mushrooms and oregano; cook for about 3 minutes or until vegetables are softened. Stir in half the cheese, serve risotto sprinkled with remaining cheese.

Serves 2.
- Not suitable to freeze.
- Suitable to microwave.
- Total fat: 21.6g.
- Fat per serve: 10.8g.

♥ ♥
ZUCCHINI LENTIL PASTIES WITH SPICY CHILLI SAUCE

Recipe can be made 3 hours ahead.

1 onion, chopped
2 cloves garlic, crushed
1 teaspoon curry powder
½ teaspoon grated fresh ginger
¼ teaspoon sambal oelek
¼ cup red lentils
⅔ cup water
1 zucchini, grated
1½ sheets (170g) ready rolled
    wholemeal pastry
1 egg white

SPICY CHILLI SAUCE
½ cup white vinegar
2 tablespoons sweet sherry
2 teaspoons salt-reduced soy sauce
½ teaspoon sambal oelek
1 teaspoon cornflour
2 teaspoons water
2 teaspoons chopped fresh parsley

Cook onion, garlic, curry powder, ginger and sambal oelek in non-stick pan for 1 minute, stir in lentils and water. Bring to boil, simmer, uncovered, for about 10 minutes or until all liquid is absorbed. Remove from heat, stir in zucchini.

Cut 6 rounds from pastry using 12cm cutter. Divide filling between rounds, fold rounds to enclose filling; pinch edges together to seal. Brush with egg white, place on baking paper-covered oven tray, bake in moderately hot oven for about 25 minutes or until well browned. Serve with sauce.

Spicy Chilli Sauce: Combine vinegar, sherry, sauce and sambal oelek in pan, stir in blended cornflour and water. Stir over heat until sauce boils and thickens. Stir in parsley.

Makes 6.
- Not suitable to freeze.
- Not suitable to microwave.
- Total fat: 39g.
- Fat per pasty: 6.5g.

♥
TEMPEH VEGETABLE BASKETS

We used 15cm square spring roll wrappers. Baskets can be made several hours ahead. Filling best cooked just before serving.

4 spring roll wrappers
1 egg white
VEGETABLE FILLING
1 tablespoon no-added-salt
    peanut butter
2 tablespoons salt-reduced soy
    sauce
200g tempeh, chopped
2 teaspoons polyunsaturated oil
1 onion, chopped
1 clove garlic, crushed
227g can bamboo shoots, rinsed,
    drained
1 red pepper, sliced
½ Chinese cabbage, shredded
2 green shallots, sliced
2 tablespoons green ginger wine
1 tablespoon salt-reduced soy
    sauce, extra
1 teaspoon cornflour
¼ cup water

Wet 2 x 30cm squares of baking paper, wrap around base and sides of 2 inverted souffle dishes (1 cup capacity); place dishes onto oven tray.

Brush spring roll wrappers lightly with egg white, layer 2 wrappers at an angle, place over a prepared dish, shape wrappers around dish. Repeat with remaining dish and wrappers.

Bake baskets in moderate oven for about 8 minutes or until lightly browned. Remove baskets from

dishes, add filling just before serving.

Vegetable Filling: Combine peanut butter and sauce in bowl, stir in tempeh, stand for several hours.

Heat oil in wok or pan, add tempeh mixture, stir-fry until lightly browned;

remove from wok. Add onion, garlic, bamboo shoots and pepper to wok, stir-fry for 1 minute. Add cabbage and shallots, stir-fry until just wilted. Stir in tempeh mixture, wine, extra sauce and blended cornflour and water, stir until mixture boils and thickens.

Serves 2.

■ Not suitable to freeze.

■ Not suitable to microwave.

■ Total fat: 27.4g.

■ Fat per serve: 13.7g.

ABOVE: Clockwise from back: Tempeh Vegetable Baskets, Zucchini Lentil Pasties with Spicy Chilli Sauce, Vegetable Risotto.

♥ ♥
MINTED VEGETABLE TERRINE

Recipe is best prepared a day ahead.

200g reduced-fat ricotta cheese
½ cup low-fat plain yogurt
2 teaspoons grated lemon rind
2 tablespoons chopped fresh mint
1 tablespoon chopped fresh parsley
1 small green cucumber, chopped
50g mushrooms, chopped
1 small carrot, chopped
1 clove garlic, crushed
3 teaspoons gelatine
¼ cup water

Rinse 8cm x 26cm bar pan in cold water. Beat cheese and yogurt in bowl with electric mixer until smooth and creamy. Stir in rind, herbs, cucumber, mushrooms, carrot and garlic.

Sprinkle gelatine over water in cup, stand in small pan of simmering water, stir until dissolved; cool slightly. Stir gelatine mixture into vegetable mixture, spoon into prepared pan, refrigerate overnight.

Serves 2.
- ■ Not suitable to freeze.
- ■ Not suitable to microwave.
- ▨ Total fat: 17g.
- ■ Fat per serve: 8.5g.

♥ ♥
HOT VEGETABLE
AND TOFU SALAD

Make recipe just before serving.

2 teaspoons polyunsaturated oil
1 onion, quartered
1 teaspoon grated fresh ginger
250g packet firm tofu, chopped
1 small carrot, sliced
1 small red pepper, sliced
100g broccoli, chopped
100g snow peas
1 stick celery, sliced
½ cup water
½ vegetable stock cube, crumbled
2 tablespoons oyster sauce
1 tablespoon salt-reduced soy sauce

Heat oil in pan, add onion and ginger, cook until onion is soft. Stir in tofu and remaining ingredients, bring to boil, simmer, uncovered, for about 5 minutes or until vegetables are tender.

Serves 2.
- ■ Not suitable to freeze.
- ■ Suitable to microwave.
- ▨ Total fat: 19.5g.
- ■ Fat per serve: 9.7g.

♥ ♥
VEGETABLE PARCELS
WITH PUMPKIN SAUCE

Parcels can be prepared 3 hours ahead. Sauce can be made a day ahead.

2 teaspoons polyunsaturated
**   margarine**
1 small leek, chopped
1 carrot, chopped
1 small red pepper, chopped
1 stick celery, chopped
100g mushrooms, chopped
½ cup frozen peas
2 tablespoons chopped fresh parsley
2 tablespoons chopped fresh basil
1 tablespoon no-added-salt
**   tomato paste**
4 spring roll wrappers
1 egg white, lightly beaten
1 tablespoon grated parmesan
**   cheese**

PUMPKIN SAUCE
150g pumpkin, chopped
1 small onion, chopped
1 cup water
½ vegetable stock cube, crumbled
2 teaspoons no-added-salt
**   tomato paste**

Heat margarine in pan, add leek, carrot, pepper and celery, cover, cook for about 15 minutes or until leek is soft. Stir in mushrooms, peas, herbs and paste, cook 5 minutes; cool.

Place quarter of the leek mixture along 1 side of a spring roll wrapper, fold in sides and roll up like a Swiss roll. Repeat with remaining leek mixture and wrappers. Place parcels on baking paper-covered oven tray, brush with egg white, sprinkle with cheese. Bake in moderate oven for about 30 minutes or until lightly browned. Serve with sauce.

Pumpkin Sauce: Combine all ingredients in pan, bring to boil, simmer, covered, for about 15 minutes or until pumpkin is soft. Blend or process pumpkin mixture until smooth, reheat if necessary.

Serves 2.
- ▨ Not suitable to freeze.
- ■ Not suitable to microwave.
- ▨ Total fat: 12.2g.
- ■ Fat per serve: 6.1g.

RIGHT: Clockwise from back: Minted Vegetable Terrine, Hot Vegetable and Tofu Salad, Vegetable Parcels with Pumpkin Sauce.

Tea-towel from The Bay Tree

♥
VEGETABLE MOUSSAKA

Make recipe just before serving.

1 large eggplant, sliced
1 tablespoon plain flour
½ cup buttermilk
½ cup skim milk
1 tablespoon skim milk powder
200g reduced fat ricotta cheese
100g sachet Scramblers, lightly
beaten
1 tablespoon chopped fresh parsley
410g can no-added-salt tomatoes
1 tablespoon chopped fresh basil
1 teaspoon castor sugar
¼ teaspoon paprika

Arrange eggplant in single layer on oven tray. Bake in moderately hot oven for 30 minutes, turning eggplant after 15 minutes; cool.

Combine flour, milks, milk powder, cheese, Scramblers and parsley in bowl. Combine undrained crushed tomatoes, basil and sugar in pan, bring to boil, simmer, uncovered, for about 15 minutes or until mixture is thick.

Layer eggplant, cheese mixture and tomato mixture in ovenproof dish (4 cup capacity), finishing with cheese mixture. Sprinkle with paprika, bake in moderate oven for about 40 minutes or until mixture is set and lightly browned.

Serves 2.
- Not suitable to freeze.
- Not suitable to microwave.
- Total fat: 30.7g.
- Fat per serve: 15.4g.

LEFT: Vegetable Moussaka.

Casserole dish, spoon and cane table from The Australian East India Co.

Carrot and Kumara Sauce: Combine all ingredients in pan, bring to boil, simmer, covered, for about 20 minutes or until vegetables are soft. Discard bay leaf. Blend or process mixture until smooth; strain.

Serves 2.
- ■ Not suitable to freeze.
- ■ Not suitable to microwave.
- □ Total fat: 5.8g.
- ■ Fat per serve: 2.9g.

♥
LENTIL PATTIES WITH YOGURT MINT SAUCE

Recipe can be made a day ahead.

½ cup red lentils
½ stick celery, chopped
1 small carrot, chopped
2 cups water
½ teaspoon ground coriander
¼ teaspoon ground cumin
¼ teaspoon dried oregano leaves
1 tablespoon chopped fresh parsley
1 cup stale breadcrumbs
2 tablespoons plain flour
1 egg white, lightly beaten
¼ cup packaged breadcrumbs
1 tablespoon polyunsaturated oil

YOGURT MINT SAUCE
½ cup low-fat plain yogurt
2 teaspoons chopped fresh mint
2 teaspoons chopped fresh parsley
1 small clove garlic, crushed
1 teaspoon lemon juice

Combine lentils, celery, carrot, water, coriander, cumin and oregano in pan, bring to boil, simmer, covered, for about 20 minutes or until mixture is thickened; cool. Stir in parsley and stale breadcrumbs. Shape mixture into 4 patties, toss in flour, dip in egg white, then packaged breadcrumbs.

Heat oil in non-stick pan, add patties, cook until well browned on both sides; drain on absorbent paper. Serve with sauce.

Yogurt Mint Sauce: Combine all ingredients in bowl; mix well.

Serves 2.
- ■ Patties suitable to freeze.
- ■ Not suitable to microwave.
- □ Total fat: 21.5g.
- ■ Fat per serve: 10.8g.

♥ ♥
ONION QUICHES

Make recipe just before serving.

2 teaspoons packaged breadcrumbs
1 teaspoon polyunsaturated margarine
3 onions, thinly sliced
1 teaspoon brown sugar
4 green shallots, chopped
2 tablespoons chopped fresh chives
100g sachet Scramblers, lightly beaten
½ cup buttermilk
1 tablespoon plain flour
1 egg white

Lightly grease 2 x 15cm quiche dishes, sprinkle with breadcrumbs.

Heat margarine in pan, add onions, cook until soft. Stir in sugar, cook further 10 minutes or until onions are very soft. Add shallots and chives; cool. Divide onion mixture between prepared dishes.

Combine Scramblers, buttermilk and flour in bowl. Beat egg white in small bowl until soft peaks form, fold into Scramblers mixture; pour over onion mixture. Bake in moderate oven for about 35 minutes or until quiches are set and lightly browned.

Serves 2.
- ■ Not suitable to freeze.
- ■ Not suitable to microwave.
- □ Total fat: 15.2g.
- ■ Fat per serve: 7.6g.

♥ ♥ ♥
TOFU DUMPLINGS WITH CARROT AND KUMARA SAUCE

Sauce can be made a day ahead. Make dumplings just before serving.

TOFU DUMPLINGS
1 cup water
2 tablespoons self-raising flour
⅓ cup polenta
½ teaspoon paprika
½ cup stale breadcrumbs
100g soft tofu, mashed
2 egg whites

CARROT AND KUMARA SAUCE
1 carrot, chopped
100g kumara, chopped
¼ teaspoon cracked black peppercorns
½ onion, chopped
1 bay leaf
1½ cups water

Tofu Dumplings: Bring water to boil in pan, add combined flour, polenta and paprika all at once. Stir vigorously over heat until mixture is thick and leaves side of pan. Combine mixture with breadcrumbs and tofu in bowl, beat with electric mixer until combined. Add egg whites, beat for about 1 minute or until mixture is glossy; stand for 10 minutes.

Drop heaped teaspoons of mixture into pan of simmering water, cook for about 5 minutes or until dumplings are cooked through; drain on absorbent paper. Serve dumplings with sauce.

ABOVE LEFT: Onion Quiches.
RIGHT: Clockwise from front: Tofu Dumplings with Carrot and Kumara Sauce, Bean and Potato Bake, Lentil Patties with Yogurt Mint Sauce.

♥ ♥ ♥

BEAN AND POTATO BAKE

Make recipe just before serving.

4 (400g) potatoes, thinly sliced
1 onion, thinly sliced
½ x 220g can Mexicana chilli beans
½ cup skim milk
¼ cup grated parmesan cheese
½ teaspoon paprika

Layer potatoes, onion and beans in 2 lightly greased ovenproof dishes (1 cup capacity). Pour milk over vegetables, sprinkle with cheese and paprika. Bake, uncovered, in moderate oven for about 25 minutes or until vegetables are soft.

Serves 2.

■ Not suitable to freeze.
■ Suitable to microwave.
□ Total fat: 9.5g.
■ Fat per serve: 4.7g.

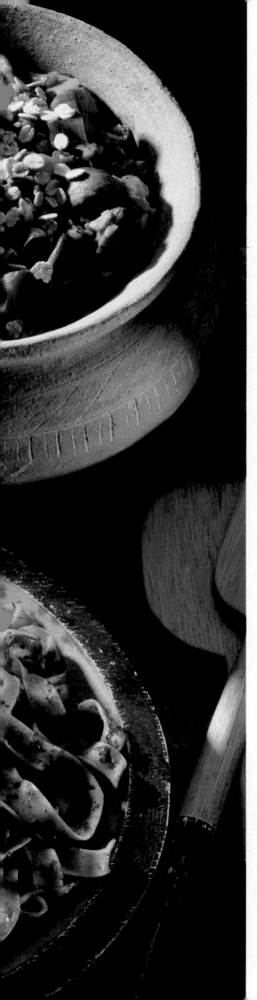

♥ TASTY VEGETABLE PIES

Pies can be prepared a day ahead.

20g polyunsaturated margarine
1 small leek, sliced
2 tablespoons plain flour
1 cup skim milk
1 zucchini, chopped
1 carrot, chopped
1 tablespoon chopped fresh parsley
½ sheet ready rolled wholemeal
 pastry
½ teaspoon skim milk, extra
½ teaspoon grated parmesan
 cheese

Heat margarine in pan, stir in leek, cook until soft. Stir in flour, cook until bubbling. Remove from heat, gradually stir in milk, stir over heat until sauce boils and thickens; cover, cool to room temperature.

Boil, steam or microwave zucchini and carrot until just tender. Stir vegetables and parsley into sauce. Spoon into 2 ovenproof dishes (1 cup capacity).

Cut pastry into 2 rounds large enough to cover dishes, brush with extra milk, sprinkle with cheese. Bake in moderately hot oven for about 20 minutes or until pastry is lightly browned and crisp.

Serves 2.
■ Not suitable to freeze.
■ Not suitable to microwave.
■ Total fat: 33.6g.
■ Fat per serve: 16.8g.

♥ ♥ ♥ RED RICE, BARLEY AND MUSHROOM CASSEROLES

Make recipe just before serving.

1 onion, sliced
200g mushrooms, chopped
1 small leek, chopped
1 apple, chopped
2 tablespoons chopped fresh basil
1 tomato, chopped
⅓ cup red rice
430g can chicken consomme
2 green shallots, chopped
½ cup rolled barley
2 teaspoons rolled barley, extra

Combine onion, mushrooms, leek, apple, basil, tomato and rice in bowl. Spoon mixture into 2 ovenproof dishes (2 cup capacity). Divide consomme evenly between dishes, cover, cook in moderate oven for about 40 minutes or until rice is tender. Stir shallots and barley into casseroles, cover, stand for 5 minutes before serving. Serve sprinkled with extra barley.

Serves 2.
■ Not suitable to freeze.
■ Suitable to microwave.
■ Total fat: 1.5g.
■ Fat per serve: Negligible.

♥ PASTA WITH PESTO SAUCE

Cook recipe just before serving.

2 cups fresh basil leaves
1 clove garlic, crushed
⅓ cup grated parmesan cheese
1 tablespoon olive oil
1 tablespoon No Oil Light French
 Dressing
275g pasta

Blend or process basil, garlic, cheese, oil and dressing until well combined.

Add pasta to large pan of boiling water, boil, uncovered, until just tender; drain. Toss pesto through pasta before serving.

Serves 2.
■ Not suitable to freeze.
■ Not suitable to microwave.
■ Total fat: 34.2g.
■ Fat per serve: 17.1g.

LEFT: Clockwise from front: Pasta with Pesto Sauce, Tasty Vegetable Pies, Red Rice, Barley and Mushroom Casseroles.

♥ ♥
SPICY BEAN CASSEROLE

Recipe can be made a day ahead

½ cup dried red kidney beans
½ cup dried lima beans
2 teaspoons polyunsaturated
   margarine
1 Spanish red onion, sliced
1 carrot, sliced
1 small red pepper, chopped
1 clove garlic, crushed
1 small fresh red chilli, chopped
1 teaspoon ground cumin
½ teaspoon ground cinnamon
½ teaspoon ground nutmeg
410g can no-added-salt tomatoes
½ cup water
½ vegetable stock cube, crumbled
2 teaspoons no-added-salt
   tomato paste
2 teaspoons honey
½ cup canned no-added-salt corn
   kernels, drained

Cover beans with water in bowl, stand overnight; drain.

Heat margarine in pan, add onion, carrot, pepper, garlic and chilli, cook until onion is soft. Stir in cumin, cinnamon and nutmeg, cook further minute. Stir in beans, undrained crushed tomatoes, water, stock cube, paste and honey.

Bring to boil, simmer, covered, for about 45 minutes, stirring occasionally, or until beans are tender. Stir in corn, simmer further 5 minutes.
   Serves 2.
■ Not suitable to freeze.
■ Suitable to microwave.
   Total fat: 13.5g.
■ Fat per serve: 6.8g.

♥ ♥ ♥
CURRIED VEGETABLE HOT POT

Curry can be made 3 hours ahead.

¼ cup water
1 teaspoon ground cumin
1 teaspoon ground coriander
1 teaspoon garam masala
1 teaspoon curry powder
410g can no-added-salt tomatoes
1¾ cups water, extra
2 potatoes, chopped
1 onion, chopped
2 carrots, chopped
500g cauliflower, chopped
½ cup fresh or frozen peas
375g broccoli, chopped
2 zucchini, chopped

Heat water in pan, stir in spices, simmer until mixture is reduced by half. Add undrained crushed tomatoes, extra water, potatoes, onion, carrots and cauliflower. Bring to boil, simmer, covered, for about 10 minutes or until potato is just soft. Add peas, broccoli and zucchini, simmer, covered, further 5 minutes or until liquid is reduced slightly and vegetables are soft.
   Serves 2.
■ Not suitable to freeze.
■ Suitable to microwave.
   Total fat: Negligible

BELOW: From top: Spicy Bean Casserole, Curried Vegetable Hot Pot.
RIGHT: Black-Eyed Bean Soup with Pinwheel Damper.

Below: Serving ware from Dansab. Right: Tea-towel and spoon from The Bay Tree.

♥
BLACK-EYED BEAN SOUP WITH PINWHEEL DAMPER

Soup can be made a day ahead. Make damper just before serving.

½ cup black-eyed beans
2 teaspoons polyunsaturated
   margarine
1 onion, chopped
1 carrot, chopped
150g kumara, chopped
1 small turnip, chopped
1 stick celery, chopped
1 zucchini, chopped
410g can no-added-salt tomatoes
1 cup water
½ vegetable stock cube, crumbled
1 teaspoon no-added-salt
   tomato paste

PINWHEEL DAMPER
2 teaspoons polyunsaturated
   margarine
6 green shallots, chopped
¼ cup chopped fresh parsley
1 cup white self-raising flour
½ cup wholemeal self-raising flour
1 teaspoon sugar
¼ cup skim milk
⅓ cup water, approximately
1 egg white, lightly beaten

Cover beans with water in bowl, stand overnight; drain.

Heat margarine in pan, add onion, carrot, kumara, turnip and celery, cook for 5 minutes. Add beans, zucchini, undrained crushed tomatoes, water, stock cube and paste. Bring to boil, simmer, covered, for about 45 minutes or until beans are tender. Serve with pinwheel damper.

Pinwheel Damper: Heat margarine in pan, add shallots and parsley, cook for 1 minute; cool.

Sift flours and sugar into bowl, stir in milk and enough water to make a sticky dough. Turn dough onto floured surface, knead gently until smooth.

Roll dough to 20cm x 30cm rectangle, spread evenly with shallot mixture, roll up dough from long side. Cut roll into 6 slices.

Place slices cut side up in greased 18cm sandwich pan, brush tops with egg white. Bake in hot oven for about 15 minutes or until well browned.

Serves 2.
■ Not suitable to freeze.
■ Not suitable to microwave.
□ Total fat: 22.4g.
■ Fat per serve: 11.2g.

Beef & Veal

♥ ♥ ♥

VEAL CHOPS WITH TANGY LEMON SAUCE

Make recipe close to serving time.

2 x 150g veal chops

LEMON SAUCE
**1 teaspoon polyunsaturated
  margarine
1 onion, sliced
2 tablespoons dry white wine
½ small chicken stock cube,
  crumbled
1 cup water
1 teaspoon castor sugar
1 teaspoon cornflour
1 tablespoon water, extra
1 tablespoon lemon juice
1 tablespoon chopped fresh parsley
1 teaspoon chopped fresh thyme**

Remove all visible fat from chops. Grill chops until tender; serve with tangy lemon sauce.

Tangy Lemon Sauce: Heat margarine in pan, add onion, cook until soft. Stir in wine, stock cube, water and sugar, bring to boil, simmer, uncovered, until reduced by one-third. Stir in blended cornflour and extra water, juice and herbs; stir gently until sauce boils and thickens.

Serves 2.
- ◻ Not suitable to freeze.
- ■ Not suitable to microwave.
- ◻ Total fat: 9g.
- ■ Fat per serve: 4.5g.

♥ ♥

BEEF AND BEER CASSEROLE

Make casserole close to serving time.

**400g topside steak
1½ tablespoons plain flour
2 teaspoons olive oil
1 leek, chopped
1 small red pepper, chopped
100g mushrooms, chopped
1 tomato, peeled, chopped
1 cup beer
½ cup water
2 teaspoons no-added-salt
  tomato paste
1 tablespoon chopped fresh parsley
2 teaspoons chopped fresh oregano**

Trim all visible fat from steak; slice steak into 4 pieces. Toss steak in flour. Heat oil in pan, add steak, cook until browned on both sides. Remove steak from pan; keep warm.

Add leek, pepper and mushrooms to pan, cook, covered, for about 10 minutes or until leek is soft. Add steak, tomato, beer, water and paste, bring to boil. Pour steak mixture into ovenproof dish, cover, bake in moderate oven for about 1¼ hours or until steak is tender. Stir in herbs just before serving.

Serves 2.
- ◻ Not suitable to freeze.
- ■ Not suitable to microwave.
- ◻ Total fat: 18.6g.
- ■ Fat per serve: 9.3g.

RIGHT: Clockwise from back: Veal with Marsala Sauce (recipe over page), Veal Chops with Tangy Lemon Sauce, Beef and Beer Casserole.

*Plates from Clay Things;
casserole from Polain Interiors*

♥ ♥ ♥
VEAL WITH MARSALA SAUCE

Recipe can be prepared a day ahead.

4 x 75g veal steaks
¼ cup marsala
1 tablespoon lemon juice
½ teaspoon olive oil
2 teaspoons cornflour
¾ cup water
½ small chicken stock cube, crumbled
3 teaspoons plum jam
1 clove garlic, crushed
3 green shallots, chopped

Remove all visible fat from veal. Pound veal thinly. Combine veal with marsala and juice in bowl, refrigerate for several hours or overnight.

Drain veal, reserve ⅓ cup marinade. Heat oil in non-stick pan, add veal, cook until tender; remove from pan.

Blend cornflour with reserved marinade in pan with water, stock cube and jam. Stir until mixture boils and thickens. Stir in garlic and shallots. Serve veal with sauce.

Serves 2.
■ Not suitable to freeze.
■ Not suitable to microwave.
□ Total fat: 7.7g.
■ Fat per serve: 3.9g.

♥ ♥ ♥
BEEF AND ONION KEBABS

Recipe is best prepared a day ahead.

350g topside steak
12 baby onions
MARINADE
¼ cup honey
¼ cup lemon juice
2 teaspoons grated fresh ginger
2 teaspoons Worcestershire sauce
¼ cup no-added-salt tomato sauce
1 tablespoon chopped fresh oregano

Remove all visible fat from steak, chop steak into bite-sized pieces. Thread steak and onions onto 6 skewers. Place kebabs in shallow dish, add marinade, refrigerate overnight.

Grill kebabs, brushing with marinade, until meat is tender.
Marinade: Combine all ingredients in bowl; mix well.

Serves 2.
■ Not suitable to freeze.
■ Not suitable to microwave.
□ Total fat: 9.6g.
■ Fat per serve: 4.8g.

RIGHT: Clockwise from back: Sherried Roast Nut of Veal, Beef and Onion Kebabs, Lemon Veal Stir-Fry with Peppers and Pecans.

Plates from Accoutrement

♥ ♥

LEMON VEAL STIR-FRY WITH PEPPERS AND PECANS

Make recipe close to serving time.

300g veal steaks, sliced
1 onion, sliced
1 red pepper, sliced
1 green pepper, sliced
1 tablespoon chopped fresh lemon grass
2 tablespoons pecans, halved
1 teaspoon grated lemon rind
2 tablespoons lemon juice
½ small chicken stock cube, crumbled
2 tablespoons salt-reduced soy sauce
1 clove garlic, crushed

Remove all visible fat from veal. Heat wok or non-stick pan, add veal, cook until browned all over. Remove veal from pan; keep warm. Add onion, peppers and lemon grass to wok, cook until vegetables are soft. Stir in nuts, cook for 1 minute. Stir in veal with combined rind, juice, stock cube, sauce and garlic, stir-fry until heated through.
　　Serves 2.
■ Not suitable to freeze.
■ Not suitable to microwave.
　Total fat: 19.4g.
■ Fat per serve: 9.7g.

♥ ♥ ♥

SHERRIED ROAST NUT OF VEAL

Recipe is best prepared a day ahead.

750g nut of veal
MARINADE
¼ cup salt-reduced soy sauce
2 teaspoons chopped fresh ginger
2 green shallots, sliced
¼ cup dry sherry
¼ cup honey
1 tablespoon orange juice
½ x 230g can sliced water chestnuts, drained

Remove all visible fat from veal. Cover veal with marinade in bowl, cover, refrigerate overnight.
　　Drain veal; reserve marinade. Place veal on rack in baking dish. Cook, covered, in hot oven for 15 minutes, reduce heat to moderate, cook, covered, for further 30 minutes or until tender. Heat reserved marinade in pan until boiling, serve with veal.
Marinade: Combine all ingredients in bowl; mix well.
　　Serves 4.
■ Suitable to freeze.
■ Not suitable to microwave.
　Total fat: 11.3g.
■ Fat per serve: 2.8g.

♥ ♥
CHILLI MEATLOAF WITH TOMATO SAUCE

Recipe can be made 3 hours ahead.

250g topside steak
¼ cup stale breadcrumbs
1 small onion, chopped
1 clove garlic, crushed
¼ teaspoon ground oregano leaves
¼ teaspoon ground cumin
¼ teaspoon ground coriander
¼ teaspoon chilli powder
2 egg whites
TOMATO SAUCE
1 teaspoon polyunsaturated oil
1 small onion, chopped
1 small clove garlic, crushed
½ x 410g can no-added-salt tomatoes
½ teaspoon brown sugar
¼ teaspoon chilli powder
1 teaspoon Worcestershire sauce

Trim all visible fat from steak. Process all ingredients until smooth, spoon mixture evenly into 2 lightly greased small loaf pans (⅔ cup capacity). Bake in moderate oven for about 45 minutes or until firm and cooked through. Serve with sauce.
Tomato Sauce: Heat oil in pan, add onion and garlic, cook until soft. Stir in undrained crushed tomatoes and remaining ingredients. Bring to boil, simmer, uncovered, until thick. Blend or process sauce until smooth.
Serves 2.
■ Meatloaf suitable to freeze.
■ Not suitable to microwave.
□ Total fat: 12.5g.
■ Fat per serve: 6.3g.

♥ ♥ ♥
BAKED CRUMBED VEAL

Recipe can be prepared a day ahead.

4 x 60g veal steaks
2 tablespoons light mayonnaise
½ cup seasoned stuffing mix

Remove all visible fat from steaks. Lightly spread each steak with mayonnaise, coat completely with stuffing mix. Place veal on oven tray, bake in hot oven for about 15 minutes or until veal is tender.
Serves 2.
■ Not suitable to freeze.
■ Not suitable to microwave.
□ Total fat: 9.5g.
■ Fat per serve: 4.8g.

♥ ♥
MEATBALLS IN VEGETABLE PAPRIKA SAUCE

Recipe can be made a day ahead.

250g topside steak
½ cup stale breadcrumbs
1 tablespoon chopped fresh parsley
1 tablespoon chopped fresh chives
1 egg white
1 teaspoon Worcestershire sauce
1 teaspoon polyunsaturated oil
1 tablespoon chopped fresh basil
SAUCE
410g can no-added-salt tomatoes
1 cup water
2 tablespoons dry red wine
1 onion, chopped
1 carrot, chopped
1 stick celery, chopped
½ teaspoon Worcestershire sauce
½ teaspoon sugar
1 teaspoon paprika

Trim all visible fat from steak, blend or process steak until minced. Combine mince, breadcrumbs, parsley, chives, egg white and sauce in bowl. Shape mixture into small meatballs.

Heat oil in non-stick pan, add meatballs, cook until well browned all over and cooked through, drain on absorbent paper. Add meatballs and basil to sauce, mix well, stir until heated through.
Sauce: Combine undrained crushed tomatoes with remaining ingredients in pan, bring to boil, simmer, uncovered, for about 20 minutes or until vegetables are soft. Blend or process sauce until smooth, return mixture to pan to reheat.
Serves 2.
■ Suitable to freeze.
■ Not suitable to microwave.
□ Total fat: 13.8g.
■ Fat per serve: 6.9g.

LEFT: Clockwise from left: Baked Crumbed Veal, Meatballs in Vegetable Paprika Sauce, Chilli Meatloaf with Tomato Sauce.

Plates from Villa Italiana; basket from Corso de Fiori

VEAL CUTLETS WITH TOMATO CORIANDER SAUCE

Make recipe close to serving time.

2 x 150g veal cutlets
2 teaspoons olive oil
2 green shallots, chopped
1 teaspoon ground cumin
1 small fresh red chilli, chopped
1 clove garlic, crushed
1 teaspoon grated fresh ginger
4 tomatoes, peeled, chopped
½ cup water
1 tablespoon no-added-salt tomato paste
1 tablespoon lime juice
2 teaspoons sugar
1 tablespoon chopped fresh coriander
2 teaspoons chopped fresh mint

Remove all visible fat from veal. Heat oil in pan, add veal, cook until lightly browned on both sides. Remove veal from pan; keep warm.

Add shallots, cumin, chilli, garlic and ginger to pan, stir over heat for 2 minutes. Add veal, tomatoes, water, paste, juice and sugar, bring to boil, simmer, covered, for about 10 minutes or until veal is tender. Stir in herbs.

Serves 2.
- Not suitable to freeze.
- Not suitable to microwave.
- Total fat: 14.4g.
- Fat per serve: 7.2g.

SEASONED TOPSIDE ROLL

Roll can be prepared 2 days ahead.

350g piece topside steak
2 teaspoons polyunsaturated oil
2 teaspoons plain flour
¼ cup dry red wine
¼ cup water
½ small beef stock cube, crumbled
SEASONING
½ cup rolled oats
¼ cup water
1 teaspoon polyunsaturated oil
1 small onion, chopped
1 clove garlic, crushed
2 tablespoons currants
2 tablespoons chopped fresh chives
¼ teaspoon sugar

ABOVE: Seasoned Topside Roll.
RIGHT: Clockwise from back right: Beef in Red Wine (recipe over page), Peppered Veal Medallions, Veal Cutlets with Tomato Coriander Sauce.

Above: Plate from Accoutrement; table and background screen from Corso de Fiori. Right: Serving ware from Villa Italiana

Remove all visible fat from steak. Place steak between 2 sheets of plastic. Pound out thinly to a rectangle, spread with seasoning, roll up from narrow end like a Swiss roll; secure roll with string.

Heat oil in non-stick baking dish, add roll, cook over heat until browned all over. Bake, uncovered, in moderate oven for about 20 minutes or until tender. Remove roll from dish, cover while preparing sauce.

Add flour to dish, stir over heat for about 1 minute or until well browned. Remove from heat, gradually stir in combined wine, water and stock cube. Stir over heat until sauce boils and thickens; strain. Remove string from roll, slice and serve with sauce.
Seasoning: Combine oats and water in bowl, stand 10 minutes. Heat oil in pan, add onion and garlic, cook until soft. Combine onion mixture, oat mixture, currants, chives and sugar in bowl.

Serves 2.
- Suitable to freeze.
- Not suitable to microwave.
- Total fat: 26.6g.
- Fat per serve: 13.3g.

PEPPERED VEAL MEDALLIONS

Make recipe just before serving.

4 x 80g veal medallions
2 tablespoons canned drained green peppercorns, crushed
¼ cup brandy
½ cup buttermilk

Remove all visible fat from veal. Combine veal, peppercorns and brandy in bowl; refrigerate for several hours or overnight.

Drain veal, reserve marinade. Cook veal in heated non-stick pan until tender. Remove from pan; keep warm. Combine reserved marinade and buttermilk in pan, bring to boil, pour over veal just before serving.

Serves 2.
- Not suitable to freeze.
- Not suitable to microwave.
- Total fat: 8.5g.
- Fat per serve: 4.3g.

♥ ♥
BEEF IN RED WINE

Recipe can be made a day ahead.

350g blade steak
2 onions, chopped
1 clove garlic, crushed
½ small green pepper, chopped
1 stick celery, chopped
2 carrots, chopped
100g mushrooms, sliced
415ml can tomato puree
2 teaspoons Worcestershire sauce
½ cup dry red wine
1 teaspoon dried mixed herbs

Trim all visible fat from steak, cut steak into cubes. Combine steak with remaining ingredients in pan, bring to boil, simmer, covered, for about 1½ hours, or until steak is tender.
　　Serves 2.
■　Not suitable to freeze.
■　Not suitable to microwave.
　　Total fat: 15g.
■　Fat per serve: 7.5g.

♥ ♥ ♥
BEEF AND MUSHROOM CASSEROLE

Recipe can be made a day ahead.

350g chuck steak
1 tablespoon plain flour
¼ cup water
100g baby mushrooms
100g baby onions
½ cup dry red wine
1 cup water, extra
1 tablespoon no-added-salt tomato paste
1 bay leaf

Remove all visible fat from steak, cut steak into bite-sized pieces. Toss steak in flour. Heat water in pan, stir in steak, cook for 3 minutes, stir in remaining ingredients. Bring to boil, simmer, covered, for about 1½ hours or until meat is tender. Remove bay leaf before serving.
　　Serves 2.
■　Not suitable to freeze.
■　Not suitable to microwave.
　　Total fat: 8.7g.
■　Fat per serve: 4.4g.

ABOVE: Beef and Mushroom Casserole.
RIGHT: Beef and Pear with Garlic Mustard Sauce.

Above: Bowl and plate from Clay Things.
Right: Plate from Mikasa

♥ ♥
BEEF AND PEAR WITH GARLIC MUSTARD SAUCE

Make recipe close to serving time.

1 pear, halved
¾ cup water
½ cup orange juice
350g Scotch fillet steak
½ teaspoon olive oil
2 cloves garlic, crushed
2 teaspoons seeded mustard
2 teaspoons cornflour
1 tablespoon brandy
1 clove garlic, crushed, extra

Combine pear, water and juice in pan, bring to boil, remove from heat; cool pear in liquid.
　　Remove all visible fat from steak. Heat oil in non-stick pan, add steak, cook until well browned and tender. Remove steak from pan; keep warm.
　　Drain pear, reserving 1¼ cups liquid. Add garlic and mustard to same pan, cook for 1 minute. Stir in blended cornflour and reserved liquid, stir over heat until mixture boils and thickens. Stir in brandy and extra garlic. Slice beef, serve with sliced pear and sauce.
　　Serves 2.
■　Not suitable to freeze.
■　Not suitable to microwave.
　　Total fat: 15.5g.
■　Fat per serve: 7.8g.

Lamb

♥ ♥ LAMB LOIN WITH HAZELNUT CHIVE CRUST

Recipe can be prepared 3 hours ahead.

700g loin of lamb, boned
8 English spinach leaves
½ cup stale breadcrumbs
¼ cup chopped roasted unsalted hazelnuts
¼ cup chopped fresh chives
2 tablespoons port
1 tablespoon chutney

Trim all visible fat from lamb, open lamb flat on bench.

Drop spinach in boiling water for 30 seconds, rinse in cold water, drain; pat dry with absorbent paper. Place spinach over lamb, roll lamb tightly; secure with skewers.

Combine remaining ingredients in bowl, press firmly over surface of lamb. Place lamb on rack in baking dish, bake in moderate oven for about 1 hour or until tender.

Serves 4.
- ■ Suitable to freeze.
- ■ Not suitable to microwave.
- □ Total fat: 28g.
- ■ Fat per serve: 7g.

♥ ♥ LAMB FILLETS WITH VEGETABLE SAUCE

Make recipe just before serving.

4 (300g) lamb fillets
½ cup sweet sherry
1 cup water
1 carrot, chopped
½ red pepper, chopped
1 tomato, chopped
1 stick celery, chopped
1 onion, chopped
1 tablespoon low-fat plain yogurt
1 tablespoon chopped fresh oregano
1 clove garlic, crushed

LEFT: Lamb Loin with Hazelnut Chive Crust.
ABOVE: From top: Honeyed Ginger Lamb Kebabs, Lamb Fillets with Vegetable Sauce.

Above: Basket from Polain Interiors

Trim all visible fat from lamb. Cook lamb over heat in baking dish until lamb is browned all over. Remove lamb from dish.

Add sherry and water to dish, bring to boil, remove from heat. Add carrot, pepper, tomato, celery and onion to dish, bake, covered, in moderately hot oven for about 20 minutes or until vegetables are soft.

Place lamb on vegetables, bake further 10 minutes or until lamb is tender. Remove lamb from dish; keep warm while making sauce.

Blend or process vegetable mixture until smooth, push through fine sieve, stir in yogurt, oregano and garlic. Serve lamb with sauce.

Serves 2.
- ■ Not suitable to freeze.
- ■ Not suitable to microwave.
- □ Total fat: 10.8g.
- ■ Fat per serve: 5.4g.

♥ ♥ ♥ HONEYED GINGER LAMB KEBABS

Recipe is best prepared a day ahead.

750g leg of lamb, boned
MARINADE
¾ cup green ginger wine
1 tablespoon honey
¼ cup mint jelly
2 teaspoons grated fresh ginger
2 teaspoons salt-reduced soy sauce

Trim all visible fat from lamb, cut lamb into cubes. You should have 300g of lamb.

Thread lamb onto 6 skewers. Place kebabs in shallow dish, add marinade; refrigerate overnight.

Grill kebabs, brushing with marinade, until tender.

Marinade: Combine all ingredients in bowl; mix well.

Serves 2.
- ■ Not suitable to freeze.
- ■ Not suitable to microwave.
- □ Total fat: 6.6g.
- ■ Fat per serve: 3.3g.

♥ ♥

LAMB KIBBE WITH TAHINI SAUCE

Make recipe close to serving time. Sauce can be made 3 hours ahead.

¼ cup burghul
250g lamb leg chops
1 small onion, chopped
3 teaspoons chopped pine nuts
1 egg white
2 tablespoons chopped fresh parsley
1 tablespoon chopped fresh mint
½ teaspoon dried oregano leaves
¼ teaspoon dried basil leaves

TAHINI SAUCE
2 tablespoons low-fat plain yogurt
1 teaspoon tahini paste
1 teaspoon salt-reduced soy sauce
1 teaspoon chopped fresh parsley

Grease deep 15cm square cake pan. Cover burghul with cold water in bowl, stand for 1 hour, drain; squeeze out excess moisture.

Trim all visible fat from lamb, blend or process lamb until minced. Combine lamb, onion, nuts, egg white, parsley, mint, oregano and basil in bowl; press mixture into prepared pan. Bake in moderate oven for about 40 minutes or until cooked through. Cut into 4 squares, serve with tahini sauce.

Tahini Sauce: Combine all ingredients in bowl; mix well.

Serves 2.
■ Kibbe suitable to freeze.
■ Not suitable to microwave.
■ Total fat: 16.5g.
■ Fat per serve: 8.3g.

RIGHT: Clockwise from front: Lamb Hot Pot with Couscous, Lamb and Yogurt Curry (recipe over page), Lamb Kibbe with Tahini Sauce.
FAR RIGHT: Lamb Fillets in Herb Marinade.

Far right: Plate from Clay Things

♥ LAMB HOT POT WITH COUSCOUS

Hot pot can be made several hours ahead. Couscous is best made close to serving time.

600g lamb leg chops
1 tablespoon plain flour
2 teaspoons olive oil
1 onion, sliced
1 teaspoon ground cinnamon
1 teaspoon turmeric
1½ cups water
½ small beef stock cube, crumbled
100g prunes, pitted
COUSCOUS
2 cups boiling water
1 cup couscous

Trim all visible fat from lamb, cut lamb into cubes; toss in flour.

Heat oil in pan, add onion, cook until soft. Add lamb, cook until lamb is browned all over. Stir in cinnamon and turmeric, cook 1 minute. Stir in water, stock cube and prunes, bring to boil, simmer, covered, for about 30 minutes or until lamb is tender. Serve lamb with couscous.

Couscous: Pour water over couscous in bowl, stand for 5 minutes or until liquid is absorbed, stir with a fork.

Serves 2.

■ Not suitable to freeze.
■ Not suitable to microwave.
□ Total fat: 28.8g.
■ Fat per serve: 14.4g.

♥ ♥ LAMB FILLETS IN HERB MARINADE

Recipe best prepared 3 hours ahead.

300g lamb fillets
2 teaspoons cracked black peppercorns
HERB MARINADE
2 teaspoons polyunsaturated oil
1½ tablespoons tarragon vinegar
1 tablespoon water
2 teaspoons sugar
1 teaspoon drained canned green peppercorns
¼ teaspoon dry mustard
2 green shallots, chopped
2 teaspoons chopped fresh parsley
1 teaspoon chopped fresh thyme

Trim all visible fat from fillets. Press peppercorns onto fillets. Place fillets onto greased oven tray, bake in moderately hot oven for about 25 minutes or until tender, drain on absorbent paper; cool.

Slice lamb, place in bowl, cover with marinade, refrigerate for several hours before serving.

Herb Marinade: Combine all ingredients in bowl; mix well.

Serves 2.

■ Not suitable to freeze.
■ Not suitable to microwave.
□ Total fat: 19.8g.
■ Fat per serve: 9.9g.

Spoon topping mixture into large piping bag fitted with a fluted tube; pipe onto pie. Bake in moderate oven for about 40 minutes or until topping is lightly browned.

Topping: Boil, steam or microwave potatoes until soft. Mash potatoes in bowl until free of lumps. Beat potatoes and milk with electric mixer until light and fluffy.

Serves 2.
- Not suitable to freeze.
- Not suitable to microwave.
- Total fat: 24g.
- Fat per serve: 12g.

♥ ♥

CRUMBED LAMB WITH ONION MARMALADE

Marmalade can be made 3 days ahead. Cook lamb just before serving.

4 x 75g lamb fillets
½ cup stale breadcrumbs
1 tablespoon chopped fresh parsley
¼ teaspoon paprika
½ teaspoon olive oil
ONION MARMALADE
2 onions, sliced
¾ cup water
1 teaspoon grated orange rind
¼ cup orange juice
¼ cup brown vinegar
⅓ cup brown sugar

Trim fat from lamb. Roll lamb in combined breadcrumbs, parsley and paprika; press crumbs on firmly.

Brush small oven tray with the oil, place lamb on tray, bake in moderately hot oven for about 10 minutes or until cooked as desired. Serve lamb with onion marmalade.

Onion Marmalade: Combine onions and water in pan, cook, covered, for about 15 minutes or until very soft. Add rind, juice, vinegar and sugar, stir over heat until sugar is dissolved. Bring to boil, simmer, uncovered, for about 30 minutes or until thick.

Serves 2.
- Not suitable to freeze.
- Not suitable to microwave.
- Total fat: 13g.
- Fat per serve: 6.5g.

♥ ♥ ♥

LAMB AND YOGURT CURRY

Recipe can be made a day ahead.

750g leg of lamb, boned
1 large onion, chopped
1 teaspoon grated fresh ginger
1 clove garlic, crushed
1 teaspoon chilli powder
1 teaspoon ground coriander
2 teaspoons ground cumin
½ teaspoon ground black pepper
1 teaspoon garam masala
1 teaspoon dry mustard
1 teaspoon turmeric
¼ teaspoon ground cardamom
2 tablespoons lemon juice
1 cup water
½ cup low-fat plain yogurt

Trim all visible fat from lamb; cut lamb into cubes. You should have 300g of lamb.

Combine lamb and remaining ingredients, except yogurt, in pan. Simmer, covered, for about 1½ hours, or until meat is tender and liquid is reduced by half; stir in yogurt.

Serves 2.
- Suitable to freeze.
- Suitable to microwave.
- Total fat: 6.6g.
- Fat per serve: 3.3g.

♥

SHEPHERD'S PIE

Pie can be made 2 days ahead.

750g lamb chump chops
1 teaspoon olive oil
1 onion, chopped
1 carrot, chopped
¾ cup water
1 tablespoon no-added-salt tomato paste
1 teaspoon salt-reduced soy sauce
1 teaspoon Worcestershire sauce
½ small chicken stock cube, crumbled
1 tablespoon plain flour
2 tablespoons water, extra
TOPPING
2 large (500g) potatoes, chopped
¼ cup skim milk

Remove lamb from bones, trim all visible fat from lamb (you should have about 300g lean meat). Blend or process lamb until minced.

Heat oil in pan, stir in mince, onion and carrot, stir until mince is browned all over. Stir in water, paste, sauces and stock cube, bring to boil, simmer, uncovered, for 5 minutes. Stir in blended flour and extra water, stir until mixture boils and thickens. Spoon into ovenproof dish (3 cup capacity).

ABOVE: Shepherd's Pie.
RIGHT: Crumbed Lamb with Onion Marmalade.

Right: Plate from Accoutrement; plant from Liquidamber Nursery.

Pork

♥
OATY PORK WITH APPLE AND PEPPERCORN SAUCE

Pork can be prepared several hours ahead. Sauce is best made close to serving time.

2 x 200g pork medallions
1 tablespoon plain flour
1 egg white, lightly beaten
½ cup rolled oats
3 teaspoons olive oil
APPLE AND PEPPERCORN SAUCE
⅔ cup water
1 tablespoon dry white wine
½ small chicken stock cube, crumbled
1 apple, sliced
2 teaspoons cornflour
1 tablespoon water, extra
1 teaspoon drained canned green peppercorns, crushed

Trim all visible fat from pork. Toss pork in flour, dip in egg white, then oats. Press oats firmly onto pork; refrigerate for 30 minutes.

Heat oil in pan, add pork, cook until browned and tender. Serve with sauce.

Apple and Peppercorn Sauce: Combine water, wine and stock cube in pan, bring to boil, add apple, simmer, covered, until apple is tender. Remove apple from pan, drain on absorbent paper. Stir blended cornflour and extra water into pan, stir until mixture boils and thickens. Stir in peppercorns and apple.

Serves 2.
◻ Not suitable to freeze.
■ Not suitable to microwave.
◻ Total fat: 23.6g.
■ Fat per serve: 11.8g.

RIGHT: Clockwise from front: Rosemary Pork with Mandarin Sauce, Apricot and Mint Pork Medallions, Oaty Pork with Apple and Peppercorn Sauce.

China from Accoutrement; plant from Liquidamber Nursery

♥ ♥
ROSEMARY PORK
WITH MANDARIN SAUCE

You will need 2 mandarins for this recipe. Recipe is best made close to serving time.

300g pork fillet
2 teaspoons olive oil
½ cup water
1 tablespoon Grand Marnier
½ small chicken stock cube, crumbled
2 teaspoons cornflour
1 tablespoon water, extra
½ cup mandarin juice
2 teaspoons chopped fresh rosemary

Trim all visible fat from pork. Heat oil in pan, add pork, cook until browned all over. Place pork on rack in baking dish.

Add water, liqueur and stock cube to pan, bring to boil, pour into baking dish. Bake, covered, in moderate oven for about 20 minutes or until pork is tender. Remove pork from rack; keep warm.

Stir in combined blended cornflour and extra water with juice into dish, stir over heat until mixture boils and thickens, stir in rosemary. Serve pork with sauce.

Serves 2.
◻ Not suitable to freeze.
◼ Not suitable to microwave.
◻ Total fat: 14.1g.
◼ Fat per serve: 7g.

♥ ♥ ♥
APRICOT AND MINT
PORK MEDALLIONS

Recipe best made just before serving.

4 x 80g pork medallions
425g can apricot halves, drained
1 tablespoon chopped fresh mint

Trim all visible fat from pork. Cut a pocket along 1 side of each medallion.

Chop half the apricots, blend or process remaining apricots until smooth; reserve apricot puree. Fill pockets with combined chopped apricots and mint; secure openings with toothpicks.

Cook pork in heated non-stick pan, brushing with reserved apricot puree, until well browned and tender. Serve pork with remaining hot apricot puree.

Serves 2.
◻ Not suitable to freeze.
◼ Not suitable to microwave.
◻ Total fat: 7g.
◼ Fat per serve: 3.5g.

♥ ♥ ♥
PORK WITH CHERRY SAUCÉ

Sauce can be made a day ahead. Pork is best cooked just before serving.

2 x 200g pork butterfly steaks
1 teaspoon polyunsaturated oil
CHERRY SAUCE
½ x 425g can pitted black cherries
2 teaspoons cornflour
1 tablespoon water
1 teaspoon port
½ teaspoon grated lemon rind

Trim all visible fat from pork. Heat oil in non-stick pan, add pork, cook until well browned and tender. Serve pork with cherry sauce.

Cherry Sauce: Drain cherries, reserve syrup. Combine reserved syrup and blended cornflour and water in pan, stir over heat until mixture boils and thickens, stir in cherries, port and rind, stir until heated through.

Serves 2.
■ Not suitable to freeze.
■ Not suitable to microwave.
 Total fat: 6.5g.
■ Fat per serve: 3.3g.

RIGHT: Clockwise from back left: Pork in Pastry with Cucumber Salad, Pork and Apple Kebabs (recipe over page), Chilli Pork and Bean Feast.
BELOW: Pork with Cherry Sauce.

Below: Plate from Clay Things

♥ ♥ ♥
PORK IN PASTRY WITH CUCUMBER SALAD

Pork is best prepared close to serving time. Cucumber salad can be made a day ahead.

300g pork fillet
1 tablespoon mint jelly
4 sheets fillo pastry
CUCUMBER SALAD
3 small green cucumbers, sliced
1 tablespoon cider vinegar
1 tablespoon chopped fresh mint
1 tablespoon mint jelly
2 teaspoons salt-reduced soy sauce
1 tablespoon dry sherry

Trim all visible fat from pork. Cut pork lengthways into 4 strips, combine with jelly, refrigerate 2 hours.

Fold a sheet of pastry in half. Place 1 piece of pork diagonally across pastry, roll up firmly, twist ends to seal. Repeat with remaining pork and pastry. Place pork on oven tray, bake in moderately hot oven for about 15 minutes or until pastry is well browned and meat is tender. Serve with cucumber salad.

Cucumber Salad: Combine cucumbers, vinegar, mint, jelly, sauce and sherry in bowl; refrigerate 2 hours.

Serves 2.
■ Not suitable to freeze.
■ Not suitable to microwave.
 Total fat: 5g.
■ Fat per serve: 2.5g.

♥ ♥ ♥
CHILLI PORK AND BEAN FEAST

Recipe can be made 2 days ahead.

600g pork butterfly steaks
1 teaspoon polyunsaturated oil
1 clove garlic, crushed
1 onion, chopped
1 cup water
410g can no-added-salt tomatoes
1 green pepper, chopped
1 tablespoon no-added-salt
** tomato paste**
½ teaspoon chilli powder
½ teaspoon ground cumin
½ teaspoon ground coriander
310g can red kidney beans,
** rinsed, drained**

Trim all visible fat from pork (you should have 300g trimmed meat). Blend or process pork until minced.

Heat oil in pan, add garlic and onion, cook until soft. Stir in pork, stir until browned all over. Stir in water, undrained crushed tomatoes, pepper, paste, chilli, cumin and coriander. Bring to boil, simmer, uncovered, for 30 minutes. Stir in beans, stir until heated through.

Serves 2.
■ Not suitable to freeze.
■ Not suitable to microwave.
 Total fat: 7.5g.
■ Fat per serve: 3.8g.

♥ ♥ ♥

PORK AND APPLE KEBABS

Recipe is best prepared a day ahead.

300g pork fillet
½ cup honey
¼ cup salt-reduced soy sauce
1 teaspoon chilli sauce
1 clove garlic, crushed
1 teaspoon grated fresh ginger
2 tablespoons lemon juice
2 apples, chopped

Trim all visible fat from pork, cut pork into cubes. Combine pork, honey, sauces, garlic, ginger and juice in bowl; refrigerate for several hours or overnight.

Thread pork and apples alternately onto skewers. Grill kebabs, brushing with marinade, until tender.

Serves 2.
■ Not suitable to freeze.
■ Not suitable to microwave.
□ Total fat: 5g.
■ Fat per serve: 2.5g.

♥ ♥

PORK WITH PORT
AND MUSHROOM SAUCE

Make recipe close to serving time.

2 x 150g pork butterfly steaks
PORT AND MUSHROOM SAUCE
1 small onion, chopped
½ stick celery, chopped
½ small chicken stock cube,
    crumbled
1 cup water
2 teaspoons polyunsaturated
    margarine
2 teaspoons plain flour
¼ cup water, extra
1 teaspoon Worcestershire sauce
2 tablespoons port
100g small mushrooms

Trim all visible fat from pork. Grill pork until well browned and tender. Serve pork with port and mushroom sauce.
Port and Mushroom Sauce: Combine onion, celery, stock cube and water in pan, bring to boil, simmer, uncovered, for about 5 minutes or until liquid is reduced by half, strain; reserve liquid.

Heat margarine in pan, add flour, cook until bubbling. Remove from heat, gradually stir in reserved liquid, extra water, sauce, port and mushrooms, stir over heat until sauce boils and thickens.

Serves 2.
■ Not suitable to freeze.
■ Not suitable to microwave.
□ Total fat: 11g.
■ Fat per serve: 5.5g.

♥ ♥ ♥

STIR-FRIED PORK
WITH BLACK BEANS

Make recipe just before serving.

200g pork fillet, thinly sliced
1 egg white, lightly beaten
1 tablespoon dry sherry
2 tablespoons salt-reduced
    soy sauce
400g broccoli
1 bunch bok choy
½ cup cold water
1 leek, chopped
250g green beans, chopped
250g fresh asparagus, chopped
1 tablespoon fresh black beans
½ cup boiling water
2 tablespoons honey
1 tablespoon brown vinegar
1 tablespoon salt-reduced soy
    sauce, extra
1 teaspoon grated fresh ginger
2 teaspoons cornflour

Trim all visible fat from pork. Combine pork, egg white, sherry and sauce in bowl; refrigerate overnight.

Cook pork in heated non-stick pan, until well browned and tender; remove from pan.

Slice broccoli and bok choy stems lengthways into thin strips. Chop broccoli heads, shred bok choy leaves. Boil, steam or microwave stems until just soft, drain.

Heat cold water in pan or wok, add leek, cook until soft. Add green beans, asparagus and broccoli, stir until beans are just tender. Mash black beans with boiling water in bowl until smooth, stir in honey, vinegar, extra sauce, ginger and cornflour.

Add pork with black bean mixture to wok, stir-fry over heat until mixture boils and thickens, toss through bok choy leaves. Serve pork mixture over broccoli and bok choy stems.

Serves 2.
■ Not suitable to freeze.
■ Not suitable to microwave.
□ Total fat: 3.4g.
■ Fat per serve: 1.7g.

RIGHT: From top: Stir-Fried Pork with Black Beans, Pork with Port and Mushroom Sauce.

Vegetables

& Salads

♥ ♥ ♥
BROCCOLI AND APPLE SALAD

Make recipe close to serving time.

300g broccoli, chopped
2 apples, chopped
½ cup cider vinegar
1 tablespoon lemon juice
¾ cup apple juice
2 tablespoons honey

Boil, steam or microwave broccoli until just tender, rinse in cold water; drain. Combine broccoli and apples in bowl, stir in combined vinegar, juices and honey; refrigerate before serving.
   Serves 2.
■ Not suitable to freeze.
■ Suitable to microwave.
   Total fat: Negligible.

♥ ♥ ♥
HOT POTATO SALAD
WITH APRICOTS

Recipe can be made a day ahead.

250g baby potatoes, sliced
150g green beans, sliced
1 onion, sliced
200g cherry tomatoes
¼ cup dried apricots, sliced
DRESSING
1 teaspoon cornflour
½ cup skim milk
2 tablespoons chopped fresh mint
2 tablespoons low-fat plain yogurt

Boil, steam or microwave potatoes and beans separately until tender; drain.
   Combine potatoes, beans, onion, tomatoes and apricots in bowl. Pour dressing over just before serving.
Dressing: Blend cornflour with milk in pan, stir over heat until mixture boils and thickens. remove from heat, stir in mint; cool slightly. Stir in yogurt.
   Serves 2.
■ Not suitable to freeze.
■ Suitable to microwave.
   Total fat: Negligible.

LEFT: Clockwise from back: Broccoli and Apple Salad, Pepper and Pasta Salad (recipe over page), Hot Potato Salad with Apricots.
Bowls from Clay Things

♥ ♥ ♥
PEPPER AND PASTA SALAD

Recipe can be made a day ahead.

2 red peppers, halved
1 green pepper, halved
1 cup (100g) penne pasta
4 green shallots, chopped
DRESSING
1 tablespoon lemon juice
1 tablespoon red wine vinegar
1 tablespoon honey
1 teaspoon chopped fresh dill

Remove seeds from peppers, place peppers on oven tray, skin side up. Cook under hot grill until skins are blistered; peel away skins carefully, slice peppers thinly.

Add pasta to large pan of boiling water, boil, uncovered, until just tender; drain. Combine peppers, pasta and shallots in bowl, add dressing.
Dressing: Combine all ingredients in bowl; mix well.

Serves 2.
■ Not suitable to freeze.
■ Not suitable to microwave.
□ Total fat: 1.3g.
■ Fat per serve: Negligible.

♥ ♥ ♥
HERBED RICE MOULD

Recipe can be made 3 hours ahead.

1 cup brown rice
6 cherry tomatoes, halved
¼ cup chopped fresh parsley
¼ cup chopped fresh chives
1 tablespoon chopped fresh thyme
1 teaspoon olive oil
2 tablespoons lemon juice

Grease a mould (3 cup capacity). Add rice to pan of boiling water, boil, uncovered, for about 35 minutes or until rice is tender, drain; cool.

Arrange tomatoes over base of prepared mould. Combine rice, parsley, chives, thyme, oil and juice in bowl. Spoon rice mixture over tomatoes. Press rice mixture firmly into mould. Turn onto plate before serving.

Serves 2.
■ Not suitable to freeze.
■ Not suitable to microwave.
□ Total fat: 8.5g.
■ Fat per serve: 4.3g.

RIGHT: From top: Herbed Rice Mould, Confetti Coleslaw, Green Peas with Leek and Mushrooms.
FAR RIGHT: Lima Beans with Okra.

Right: China and cutlery from Limoges; table from The Country Trader

♥ ♥ ♥
CONFETTI COLESLAW

Make recipe close to serving time.

1 cup shredded cabbage
1 cup shredded red cabbage
1 small carrot, grated
2 green shallots, chopped
1 tablespoon light mayonnaise
1 tablespoon water

Combine all ingredients in bowl.
Serves 2.
■ Not suitable to freeze.
Total fat: 2.6g.
■ Fat per serve: 1.3g.

♥ ♥ ♥
GREEN PEAS WITH LEEK
AND MUSHROOMS

Make recipe close to serving time.

150g peas
½ leek, sliced
½ vegetable stock cube, crumbled
¾ cup water
100g baby mushrooms
1 tablespoon chopped fresh mint

Combine peas, leek, stock cube and
water in pan, bring to boil, simmer,
covered, until peas are tender. Stir in
mushrooms, simmer, covered, until
mushrooms are just tender. Stir in mint
just before serving.
Serves 2.
■ Not suitable to freeze.
■ Suitable to microwave.
Total fat: Negligible.

♥ ♥ ♥
LIMA BEANS WITH OKRA

Recipe can be made a day ahead.

1 cup (200g) dried lima beans
1 onion, chopped
1 clove garlic, crushed
410g can no-added-salt tomatoes
1 cup water
½ small chicken stock cube,
  crumbled
500g okra
2 tablespoons brown vinegar
1 tomato, chopped
2 tablespoons chopped fresh parsley
1 clove garlic, crushed, extra

Place beans in bowl, cover with hot
water, stand for several hours or
overnight; drain.
Combine beans, onion, garlic,
undrained crushed tomatoes, water
and stock cube in pan, bring to boil,
simmer, covered, for 40 minutes or
until beans are tender.
Top and tail okra, rinse well; drain.
Stir okra and vinegar into pan, simmer,
covered, further 10 minutes. Stir in
tomato, parsley and extra garlic, stir
until heated through.
Serves 2.
■ Not suitable to freeze.
■ Not suitable to microwave.
Total fat: 3.2g.
■ Fat per serve: 1.6g.

♥ ♥ ♥
ZUCCHINI POTATO FRITTATA

Make recipe just before serving.

**2 large (500g) potatoes
1 zucchini
2 tablespoons chopped fresh parsley
1 teaspoon polyunsaturated oil**

Coarsely grate potatoes and zucchini; drain well on absorbent paper. Combine potatoes, zucchini and parsley in bowl.

Heat half the oil in non-stick pan. Using an eggslice, press potato mixture evenly over base of pan, cook, uncovered, for about 10 minutes or until lightly browned underneath. Turn frittata onto a plate.

Heat remaining oil in same pan, carefully slide frittata, browned-side up into pan. Cook further 10 minutes or until lightly browned underneath. Carefully transfer frittata to plate, cut into wedges.

Serves 2.
- Not suitable to freeze.
- Not suitable to microwave.
- Total fat: 4.5g.
- Fat per serve: 2.3g.

♥ ♥ ♥
MIXED VEGETABLES WITH TARRAGON VINAIGRETTE

Make recipe just before serving.

**1 small golden nugget pumpkin,
    chopped
6 baby potatoes, halved
100g snow peas**

TARRAGON VINAIGRETTE
**2 teaspoons chopped fresh tarragon
1½ tablespoons white wine vinegar
2 teaspoons olive oil
½ teaspoon cracked black pepper
¼ teaspoon sugar**

Boil, steam or microwave pumpkin, potatoes and snow peas separately until just tender; drain. Combine vegetables in bowl, add dressing.
Tarragon Vinaigrette: Combine all ingredients in jar; shake well.
Serves 2.
- Not suitable to freeze.
- Suitable to microwave.
- Total fat: 9g.
- Fat per serve: 4.5g.

RIGHT: Clockwise from back: Zucchini and Potato Frittata, Zucchini Mushroom Salad (recipe over page), Mixed Vegetables with Tarragon Vinaigrette.

Serving ware from Villa Italiana

♥ ♥ ♥
ZUCCHINI MUSHROOM SALAD

Make recipe close to serving time.

200g zucchini, sliced
150g button mushrooms, sliced
DRESSING
2 teaspoons chopped fresh mint
1 tablespoon lemon juice
1 teaspoon seeded mustard
2 tablespoons low oil coleslaw
    dressing

Combine zucchini, mushrooms and dressing in bowl, toss gently.
Dressing: Combine all ingredients in jar; shake well.
    Serves 2.
◼ Not suitable to freeze.
◻ Total fat: 1.8g.
◼ Fat per serve: Negligible.

BELOW: Couscous and Mint Salad.
RIGHT: Beans with Mint Glaze.

Below: Plate from Villa Italiana. Right: Wooden tray from The Country Trader; spoon and fork from Dansab

♥ ♥ ♥
COUSCOUS AND MINT SALAD

Salad can be made 3 hours ahead.

½ cup couscous
½ cup boiling water
½ small chicken stock cube,
    crumbled
1 small green cucumber, chopped
1 tomato, chopped
1 carrot, grated
½ small red pepper, chopped
¼ cup chopped fresh mint
2 tablespoons lemon juice
1 teaspoon olive oil

Combine couscous, water and stock cube in bowl, stand for 10 minutes until all water has been absorbed. Stir in cucumber, tomato, carrot, pepper and mint. Stir in combined juice and oil just before serving.
    Serves 2.
◼ Not suitable to freeze.
◻ Total fat: 4.5g.
◼ Fat per serve: 2.3g.

♥ ♥ ♥
BEANS WITH MINT GLAZE

Make recipe close to serving time.

800g broad beans, shelled
100g green beans, sliced
2 carrots, chopped
MINT GLAZE
3 teaspoons dry sherry
½ vegetable stock cube, crumbled
2 teaspoons cornflour
1 tablespoon water
2 teaspoons chopped fresh mint

Place vegetables in pan, with enough water to cover, bring to boil, simmer, uncovered, until just tender, drain; reserve ⅔ cup of the liquid for mint glaze. Serve vegetables with glaze.
Mint Glaze: Combine reserved liquid, sherry, stock cube and blended cornflour and water in pan. Stir over heat until mixture boils and thickens, stir in mint.
    Serves 2.
◼ Not suitable to freeze.
◼ Not suitable to microwave.
◻ Total fat: Negligible.

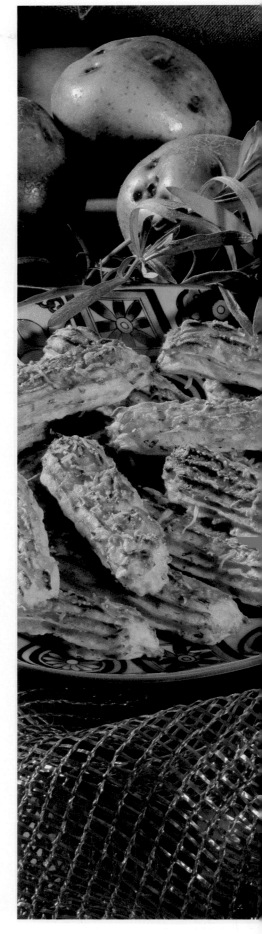

♥ ♥ ♥
CAULIFLOWER TIMBALES WITH MUSTARD SAUCE

Make recipe just before serving.

1 small red pepper
125g cauliflower, chopped
¼ cup buttermilk
2 egg whites, lightly beaten
1 tablespoon skim milk powder
1 teaspoon arrowroot
½ teaspoon sugar
MUSTARD SAUCE
1 green shallot, chopped
1 tablespoon dry white wine
1 teaspoon honey
2 teaspoons red wine vinegar
1 tablespoon lemon juice
1 teaspoon seeded mustard

Cut 2 long 1cm strips from pepper; boil, steam or microwave strips until tender; drain. Thinly slice remaining pepper; reserve for sauce.

Boil, steam or microwave cauliflower until soft; drain. Blend or process cauliflower until smooth, push through sieve (you will need ¼ cup cauliflower puree). Combine buttermilk, egg whites, skim milk powder, arrowroot and sugar in bowl. Stir in cauliflower puree.

Pour mixture into 2 wetted timbale moulds (½ cup capacity), cover each mould with foil. Place moulds into baking dish with enough boiling water to come half way up sides of moulds.

Bake in moderately hot oven for about 35 minutes or until timbales are just set, stand for 5 minutes; turn onto plates. Wrap a strip of pepper around each timbale, serve with sauce.
Mustard Sauce: Combine reserved red pepper with remaining ingredients in pan, bring to boil, remove from heat.
Serves 2.
▪ Not suitable to freeze.
▪ Not suitable to microwave.
▫ Total fat: 2.5g.
▪ Fat per serve: 1.3g.

♥ ♥ ♥
GOLDEN POTATO STICKS

Make recipe just before serving.

2 large (500g) potatoes, chopped
1 tablespoon skim milk powder
1 tablespoon chopped fresh tarragon
2 tablespoons grated fresh parmesan cheese

Boil, steam or microwave potatoes until soft, drain; mash well with fork. Stir in milk powder and tarragon. Spoon mixture into large piping bag fitted with a large fluted tube. Pipe 5cm lengths of mixture onto baking paper-covered tray, sprinkle with cheese. Bake in hot oven for about 20 minutes or until slightly puffed and browned.
Serves 2.
▪ Not suitable to freeze.
▪ Not suitable to microwave.
▫ Total fat: 6.3g.
▪ Fat per serve: 3.2g.

♥ ♥ ♥
BAKED CARROT LOAF

Make recipe just before serving.

3 medium (300g) carrots, chopped
1 onion, chopped
½ small chicken stock cube, crumbled
½ teaspoon ground black pepper
¾ cup water
100g pouch Just White Egg White Mix
¼ cup skim milk

Combine carrots, onion, stock cube, pepper and water in pan. Bring to boil, simmer, covered, until vegetables are soft; drain. Blend or process mixture until smooth, push through fine sieve; cool. Stir in egg white mix and milk.

Pour mixture into 8cm x 26cm non-stick bar pan. Bake in moderate oven for about 20 minutes or until firm.
Serves 2.
▪ Not suitable to freeze.
▪ Not suitable to microwave.
▫ Total fat: Negligible.

RIGHT: Clockwise from back: Cauliflower Timbales with Mustard Sauce, Baked Carrot Loaf, Golden Potato Sticks.

Desserts

♥ ♥ ♥

RASPBERRY APPLE TERRINE WITH ORANGE SAUCE

Recipe is best made a day ahead.

2¼ cups water
2 x 100g packets raspberry
 jelly crystals
½ cup framboise
1 teaspoon gelatine
1 tablespoon water, extra
250g punnet raspberries

APPLE JELLY
1 tablespoon gelatine
2 tablespoons water
2 cups clear apple juice

ORANGE SAUCE
20g margarine
¼ cup castor sugar
1½ cups orange juice
3 teaspoons cornflour
1 tablespoon water

Wet 11cm x 25cm loaf dish (6 cup capacity) with water, shake out excess water. Place strip of greaseproof paper into dish to cover base and extend over sides.

Heat 1 cup of the water in pan, add jelly, stir until dissolved. Stir in remaining water and liqueur. Sprinkle gelatine over extra water in cup, stand in small pan of simmering water, stir until dissolved; stir into jelly mixture.

Pour mixture into jug, pour 1 cup mixture into prepared dish, refrigerate until set. Pour in ¼ cup apple jelly mixture, arrange half the raspberries over jelly, carefully pour ¾ cup apple jelly mixture over raspberry layer; refrigerate until set.

Continue layering and refrigerating with liqueur jelly, raspberries and apple jelly. Refrigerate for several hours or overnight until set.

Unmould terrine onto plate, remove paper, serve sliced with orange sauce.

Apple Jelly: Sprinkle gelatine over water in cup, stand in small pan of simmering water, stir until dissolved. Combine with apple juice in jug.

Orange Sauce: Heat margarine in pan, stir in sugar, stir until sugar is dissolved and lightly browned. Stir in juice, stir until toffee is melted. Stir in blended cornflour and water, stir until sauce boils and thickens. Pour into jug, cover surface, cool; refrigerate until cold.

Serves 8.
■ Not suitable to freeze.
■ Not suitable to microwave.
□ Total fat: 18g.
■ Fat per serve: 2.3g.

RIGHT: Raspberry Apple Terrine with Orange Sauce.

Plates from Accoutrement

MINI ECLAIRS WITH APRICOT CREAM

You will need about 2 passionfruit for this recipe. Recipe is best made on day of serving.

CHOUX PASTRY
1 teaspoon polyunsaturated margarine
½ cup water
⅓ cup self-raising flour
2 egg whites

APRICOT CREAM
1 teaspoon gelatine
2 teaspoons water
200ml carton low-fat apricot yogurt

PASSIONFRUIT SAUCE
2 tablespoons passionfruit pulp
2 teaspoons castor sugar
1 teaspoon cornflour
2 tablespoons water

Choux Pastry: Combine margarine and water in pan, bring to boil. Add sifted flour all at once, stirring vigorously for about 30 seconds or until smooth. Transfer mixture to small bowl of electric mixer, gradually add egg whites, beating well between each addition. Mixture will separate, but will come together with further beating.

Spoon mixture into piping bag fitted with 1cm fluted tube. Pipe 6 x 7cm lengths of mixture onto non-stick oven tray. Bake in hot oven for 10 minutes, reduce heat to moderate, bake further 15 minutes or until well browned; cool.

When eclairs are cold, cut in half, scoop out any uncooked mixture; discard. Fill eclairs with apricot cream, dust with a little sifted icing sugar, if desired. Serve with sauce.

Apricot Cream: Sprinkle gelatine over water in cup, stand in small pan of simmering water; stir until dissolved. Combine yogurt and gelatine mixture in bowl, refrigerate until set.

Passionfruit Sauce: Combine passionfruit and sugar with blended cornflour and water in pan, stir over heat until sauce boils and thickens; cool.

Makes 6.
- Unfilled eclairs suitable to freeze.
- Not suitable to microwave.
- Total fat: 5.1g.
- Fat per eclair: Negligible.

WHISKY ORANGES WITH TOFFEE SAUCE

Recipe is best made a day ahead.

2 oranges
2 tablespoons whisky
½ cup castor sugar
½ cup water

Peel oranges thickly; remove all white pith from oranges. Slice oranges crossways into 4; reassemble. Place oranges into heatproof bowl, pour whisky over oranges.

Combine sugar and water in pan, stir over heat until sugar is dissolved. Bring to boil, boil for about 10 minutes or until golden brown. Allow bubbles to subside. Drizzle one-third of the toffee on lightly oiled oven tray to form mesh pattern; pour remaining toffee over oranges (toffee will bubble fiercely); refrigerate oranges overnight. Break toffee mesh into large pieces. Serve oranges with toffee sauce and toffee mesh.

Serves 2.
- Not suitable to freeze.
- Not suitable to microwave.
- Total fat: Negligible.

LINZERTORTE

Make recipe on day of serving.

¾ cup wholemeal self-raising flour
½ teaspoon ground cinnamon
2 tablespoons brown sugar
20g polyunsaturated margarine
1 tablespoon lemon juice
2 tablespoons water, approximately
⅓ cup plum jam
icing sugar

Sift flour, cinnamon and sugar into bowl, rub in margarine. Stir in juice with enough water to mix to firm dough. Turn dough onto lightly floured surface, knead lightly until smooth.

Roll three-quarters of the dough large enough to line base of shallow 19cm flan tin, spread with jam. Roll remaining dough until thin, cut into 1cm strips, place strips over jam. Bake in moderate oven for about 40 minutes or until lightly browned. Dust with sifted icing sugar; serve warm or cold.

Serves 6.
- Suitable to freeze.
- Not suitable to microwave.
- Total fat: 20.8g.
- Fat per serve: 3.5g.

ABOVE: Mini Eclairs with Apricot Cream.
RIGHT: From top: Linzertorte, Whisky Oranges with Toffee Sauce.

Above: China from The Bay Tree

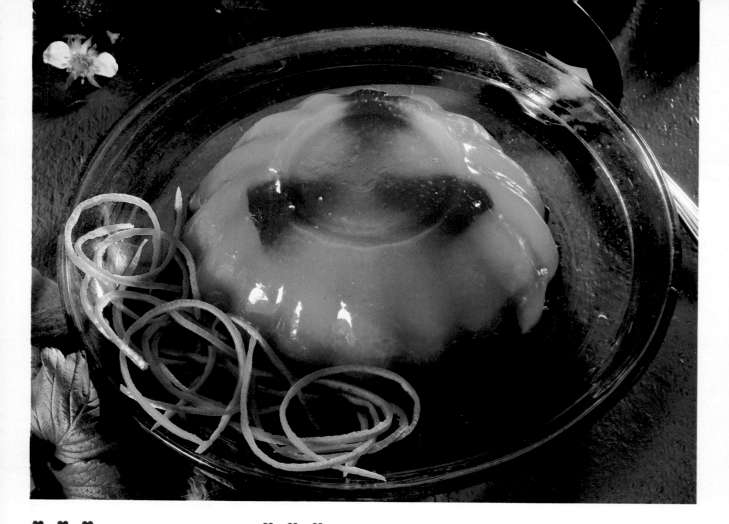

♥ ♥ ♥
APRICOT PASSIONFRUIT MOULD

You will need about 3 passionfruit for this recipe. Recipe is best prepared several hours before serving.

825g can apricots, drained
½ cup low-fat plain yogurt
¼ cup castor sugar
¼ cup passionfruit pulp
1 tablespoon gelatine
2 tablespoons water

Blend or process apricots, yogurt and sugar until smooth. Transfer mixture to bowl, fold in passionfruit. Sprinkle gelatine over water in cup, stand in small pan of simmering water, stir until dissolved, cool to room temperature; do not allow to set. Combine gelatine mixture with apricot mixture, pour into 2 glasses (1 cup capacity). Refrigerate for several hours or until set.
Serves 2.
■ Not suitable to freeze.
■ Not suitable to microwave.
■ Total fat: Negligible.

LEFT: From top: Apricot Passionfruit Mousse, Cherry Semolina Mould.
ABOVE: Fresh Orange Jelly.

Above: Plate from Accoutrement

♥ ♥ ♥
CHERRY SEMOLINA MOULD

Recipe is best prepared a day ahead.

425g can dark sweet pitted cherries
85g packet cherry jelly crystals
2 teaspoons gelatine
2 cups skim milk
2 tablespoons semolina
¼ cup castor sugar
2 tablespoons gelatine, extra
¼ cup water
2 teaspoons vanilla essence
½ cup low-fat plain yogurt

Drain cherries, reserve syrup. Bring reserved syrup to boil in pan, remove from heat, stir into combined jelly and gelatine in bowl, stir until dissolved. Stir in cherries, pour into wetted mould (4 cup capacity); refrigerate until firm.
Bring milk to boil in pan, stir in semolina and sugar, stir until mixture boils and thickens; remove from heat. Sprinkle extra gelatine over water in cup, stand in small pan of simmering water, stir until dissolved.
Stir gelatine and essence into semolina mixture; cool slightly. Stir in yogurt; cool. Pour mixture over jelly, refrigerate until set.
Serves 4.
■ Not suitable to freeze.
■ Not suitable to microwave.
■ Total fat: Negligible.

♥ ♥ ♥
FRESH ORANGE JELLY

Jelly can be made a day ahead. You will need about 3 oranges.

½ cup water
¼ cup castor sugar
1 tablespoon gelatine
¼ cup cold water, extra
1⅓ cups strained fresh orange juice
½ x 250g punnet strawberries, halved
1 orange, segmented

Combine water and sugar in pan, stir over heat until sugar is dissolved; remove from heat. Sprinkle gelatine over extra water in cup, stand in small pan of simmering water, stir until dissolved; cool slightly.
Combine gelatine mixture, sugar mixture and juice in bowl. Pour a little mixture into a mould (3 cup capacity), place a few strawberries in mould, refrigerate until set.
Repeat layering with strawberries, orange segments and juice mixture. Refrigerate until set.
Serves 2.
■ Not suitable to freeze.
■ Not suitable to microwave.
■ Total fat: Negligible.

♥ ♥ ♥
APPLE AND PEAR STRUDEL

Make strudel close to serving time.

1 apple, sliced
1 pear, sliced
1 tablespoon castor sugar
¼ teaspoon grated lemon rind
pinch ground cinnamon
2 tablespoons water
3 sheets fillo pastry

CUSTARD SAUCE
2 teaspoons custard powder
3 teaspoons castor sugar
¾ cup skim milk

Combine apple, pear, sugar, rind, cinnamon and water in pan, cook until fruit is soft; cool. Layer pastry sheets together, fold in half, spoon fruit mixture along centre of pastry, fold in ends, fold sides over fruit.

Place strudel, with folded edge down, onto baking paper-covered oven tray, bake in hot oven for 7 minutes, turn strudel over, bake further 7 minutes or until well browned. Serve with sauce.

Custard Sauce: Combine custard powder and sugar in pan, gradually stir in milk. Stir over heat until sauce boils and thickens.

Serves 2.
■ Not suitable to freeze.
■ Not suitable to microwave.
■ Total fat: Negligible.

♥ ♥ ♥
BUTTERMILK PANCAKES WITH GOLDEN PEARS

Recipe best made just before serving.

BUTTERMILK PANCAKES
1 cup self-raising flour
1 cup buttermilk
¼ cup skim milk
1 egg white

GOLDEN PEARS
2 pears, halved
¼ cup golden syrup
1 cup water
1 tablespoon lemon juice
3 teaspoons cornflour
1 tablespoon water, extra

Buttermilk Pancakes: Sift flour into bowl, gradually stir in combined milks to make a smooth batter. Beat egg white until soft peaks form, fold lightly into batter.

Pour ½ cup batter mixture into heated non-stick pan. When bubbles appear, turn pancake, cook until lightly browned underneath, remove from pan; keep warm. Repeat with remaining batter. Serve pancakes topped with pears and syrup.

Golden Pears: Place pears into pan with golden syrup, water and juice, bring to boil, simmer, uncovered, until pears are just tender. Remove pears from syrup; reserve syrup. Slice pears lengthways; serve over pancakes.

Stir blended cornflour and extra water into pan, stir over heat until mixture boils and thickens. Serve sauce over pears.

Serves 4.
■ Not suitable to freeze.
■ Not suitable to microwave.
■ Total fat: 7.5g.
■ Fat per serve: 1.9g.

RIGHT: From top: Apple and Pear Strudel, Buttermilk Pancakes with Golden Pears.

♥ ♥ ♥
BLUEBERRY TOFU ICE-CREAM

Ice-cream can be made 3 days ahead.

425g can blueberries
297g packet soft tofu
½ cup skim milk
½ cup castor sugar

Blend or process undrained blueberries, tofu, milk and sugar until smooth. Pour mixture into large loaf pan, cover, freeze for several hours or until firm.

Spoon mixture into bowl, beat with electric mixer until smooth. Return mixture to pan, cover; freeze until firm.
Serves 4.
■ Not suitable to microwave.
□ Total fat: 14.9g.
■ Fat per serve: 3.7g.

♥ ♥ ♥
SNOW EGGS WITH COFFEE CREAM

Make eggs just before serving. Coffee cream can be prepared a day ahead.

2 egg whites
2 tablespoons castor sugar
1 cup skim milk
COFFEE CREAM
2 teaspoons cornflour
1 tablespoon castor sugar
1 cup skim milk
2 teaspoons coffee and chicory
　　essence
2 teaspoons brandy

Beat egg whites in small bowl until soft peaks form. Add sugar, beat until sugar is dissolved. Bring milk to boil in shallow pan, reduce to simmer.

Using 2 dessertspoons, shape egg white mixture into ovals. Lower ovals into milk, cook for 1 minute each side, do not allow to boil or ovals will break up. Remove from pan with slotted spoon; drain. Serve snow eggs with coffee cream.
Coffee Cream: Combine cornflour and sugar in pan, gradually stir in milk. Stir over heat until sauce boils and thickens. Remove from heat, stir in essence and brandy; cool.
Serves 2.
■ Not suitable to freeze.
■ Not suitable to microwave.
□ Total fat: Negligible.

ABOVE: Snow Eggs with Coffee Cream.
RIGHT: Clockwise from back: Blueberry Tofu Ice-Cream, Pineapple Sherbet, Red Grape and Port Granita.

Above: China from Villeroy & Boch.
Right: Glasses from Sasaki

♥ ♥ ♥
PINEAPPLE SHERBET

Sherbet can be made 2 weeks ahead.

1¼kg pineapple
½ cup water
¼ cup castor sugar
1 tablespoon lemon juice
1 egg white

Peel and chop pineapple (you should have about 650g pineapple flesh).

Combine water and sugar in pan, stir over heat until sugar is dissolved. Bring to boil, simmer 1 minute; cool. Blend or process sugar syrup, pineapple and juice until combined. Pour mixture into lamington pan, cover, freeze for several hours or until firm.

Place mixture into large bowl of electric mixer or food processor with egg white; beat until creamy. Return mixture to pan, cover, freeze until firm. Allow to soften in refrigerator for 15 minutes before serving.
Serves 4.
■ Not suitable to microwave.
□ Total fat: Negligible.

♥ ♥ ♥
RED GRAPE AND PORT GRANITA

Recipe can be made a week ahead.

500g dark red grapes
2 cups water
2 tablespoons port
1 tablespoon honey
1 teaspoon grated lemon rind
½ teaspoon dark soy sauce
1 egg white

Combine grapes and water in pan, bring to boil, simmer, covered, for about 1 hour or until grapes are soft; cool. Blend or process mixture until smooth, push mixture through sieve, discard skins and seeds.

Combine grape mixture, port, honey, rind and sauce. Pour into large loaf pan, cover, freeze until just firm. Process granita until smooth, add egg white with motor operating, process until smooth and pale. Return mixture to pan, cover, freeze until firm.
Serves 2.
■ Not suitable to microwave.
□ Total fat: Negligible.

Baking

♥ ♥ ♥
CHILLI ONION TWIST

Make bread on day of serving.

7g sachet dry yeast
1 teaspoon castor sugar
¾ cup warm water
2¼ cups wholemeal plain flour
½ teaspoon salt
2 tablespoons chopped fresh chives
1 onion, chopped
3 green shallots, chopped
⅓ cup sweet chilli sauce

Combine yeast, sugar and water in bowl, cover, stand in warm place for about 10 minutes or until frothy.

Sift flour and salt into large bowl, make well in centre, stir in yeast mixture and chives, mix to a soft dough. Turn dough onto floured surface, knead for about 7 minutes until dough is smooth and elastic.

Return dough to lightly floured bowl, cover, stand in warm place for about 45 minutes or until dough is doubled in size.

Knead dough on lightly floured surface until smooth. Roll dough to 20cm x 60cm rectangle, spread with combined onion, shallots and sauce, leaving 2cm border on 1 side. Roll dough up from covered long side like a Swiss roll. Holding ends together, twist roll twice, place onto baking paper-covered oven tray. Stand, uncovered, for 20 minutes. Prick with skewer. Bake in moderately hot oven for about 30 minutes or until well browned and cooked through.

Serves 6.
- ◼ Suitable to freeze.
- ◼ Not suitable to microwave.
- ◻ Total fat: 8.4g.
- ◼ Fat per serve: 1.4g.

♥ ♥ ♥
BAPS

Make baps close to serving time.

30g compressed yeast
2 teaspoons castor sugar
⅔ cup warm water
⅔ cup warm buttermilk
3½ cups plain flour
¼ teaspoon salt
20g polyunsaturated margarine

Cream yeast and sugar in bowl, stir in water and buttermilk. Cover, stand in warm place for about 10 minutes or until mixture is frothy.

Sift flour and salt into bowl, rub in margarine; make well in centre. Stir in yeast mixture, mix to a soft dough.

Turn dough onto floured surface, knead for about 7 minutes or until dough is smooth and elastic.

Return dough to lightly oiled bowl, cover, stand in warm place for about 45 minutes or until doubled in size.

Turn dough onto lightly floured surface, knead until smooth. Divide dough into 12 portions, shape each portion into a round, place each round onto baking paper-covered oven tray; press finger firmly into centre of each round. Cover, stand in warm place for about 20 minutes or until rounds are doubled in size. Bake in moderately hot oven for about 15 minutes or until lightly browned and cooked through.

Makes 12.
- ◼ Suitable to freeze.
- ◼ Not suitable to microwave.
- ◻ Total fat: 30.2g.
- ◼ Fat per bap: 2.5g.

♥ ♥ ♥
PUMPKIN DAMPER

You will need to cook about 500g pumpkin for this recipe. Damper is best made close to serving time.

**3 cups self-raising flour
2 teaspoons polyunsaturated
   margarine
1½ cups cooked mashed pumpkin
1 tablespoon water, approximately**

Sift flour into bowl, rub in margarine. Stir in pumpkin and enough water to mix to a sticky dough. Turn dough onto lightly floured surface, knead until smooth. Place damper on non-stick oven tray, pat out to a 25cm round, cut a 1cm deep cross in surface.

Bake in hot oven for 10 minutes, reduce heat to moderate, bake further 20 minutes or until golden brown and cooked through.

Serves 8.
■ Suitable to freeze.
■ Not suitable to microwave.
□ Total fat: 16.6g.
■ Fat per serve: 2g.

♥ ♥ ♥
WHOLEMEAL CRACKERS

Crackers can be made 3 days ahead.

**½ cup wholemeal plain flour
¼ cup white plain flour
20g polyunsaturated margarine
¼ cup grated fresh parmesan cheese
pinch cayenne pepper
1 egg white, lightly beaten
2 tablespoons water, approximately**

Sift flours into bowl, rub in margarine, stir in cheese and pepper. Stir in egg white with enough water to make ingredients cling together. Turn dough onto lightly floured surface, knead until smooth. Roll dough to 18cm x 36cm rectangle, fold in half lengthways, repeat rolling and folding.

Roll dough out until 3mm thick, cut into rounds using 7cm cutter. Place rounds onto baking paper-covered oven tray, bake in moderately hot oven for about 12 minutes or until golden brown; cool on tray.

Makes 18.
■ Suitable to freeze.
■ Not suitable to microwave.
□ Total fat: 30g.
■ Fat per serve: 1.6g.

LEFT: Clockwise from back left: Pumpkin Damper, Wholemeal Crackers, Baps, Chilli Onion Twist.

Sprinkle fig mixture evenly over dough, roll up dough from long side; cut into 12 slices.

Place slices in prepared pan, bake in hot oven for about 20 minutes or until cooked through. Stand 5 minutes before turning onto wire rack to cool. Drizzle with icing when cold.

Orange Icing: Sift icing sugar into bowl, stir in rind and enough juice to give a pouring consistency.

Makes 12.
- ■ Suitable to freeze.
- ■ Not suitable to microwave.
- ■ Total fat: 25.7g.
- ■ Fat per pinwheel: 2g.

♥ ♥

CUSTARD TARTS WITH LOW-FAT SWEET PASTRY

Tarts can be made a day ahead.

LOW-FAT SWEET PASTRY
2 teaspoons polyunsaturated margarine
1 tablespoon castor sugar
¾ cup self-raising flour
1 tablespoon custard powder

CUSTARD FILLING
2 teaspoons gelatine
1 tablespoon water
1 tablespoon castor sugar
1 tablespoon custard powder
¾ cup skim milk
1 teaspoon vanilla essence

Low-Fat Sweet Pastry: Cream margarine and sugar in bowl with wooden spoon until well combined. Stir in sifted flour and custard powder in 2 batches. Knead dough on lightly floured surface until smooth. Divide dough into 2 portions, press dough, with fingers, evenly over bases and sides of 2 x 11cm non-stick pie tins.

Bake in moderate oven for about 15 minutes or until lightly browned, cool in tins. Remove pastry cases from tins, fill with custard, sprinkle with a little nutmeg, if desired. Refrigerate until custard is set.

Custard Filling: Sprinkle gelatine over water in cup, stand in small pan of simmering water, stir until dissolved. Combine sugar with custard powder in pan, gradually stir in milk, stir over heat until mixture boils and thickens. Stir in essence and gelatine mixture.

Makes 2.
- ■ Not suitable to freeze.
- ■ Not suitable to microwave.
- ■ Total fat: 10.7g.
- ■ Fat per serve: 5.4g.

♥ ♥ ♥

CRANBERRY MUFFINS

Muffins can be made a day ahead.

1 cup wholemeal self-raising flour
¾ cup oat bran
⅓ cup castor sugar
½ teaspoon ground cinnamon
⅔ cup cranberry sauce
1 egg white
20g polyunsaturated margarine, melted
⅔ cup buttermilk

Line 12-hole muffin pan with paper cases. Combine sifted flour, bran, sugar and cinnamon in bowl. Stir in sauce, egg white, margarine and buttermilk. Spoon mixture into prepared pan, bake in moderate oven for about 25 minutes or until firm.

Makes 12.
- ■ Suitable to freeze.
- ■ Not suitable to microwave.
- ■ Total fat: 31.6g.
- ■ Fat per muffin: 2.6g.

♥ ♥ ♥

FIG AND ORANGE PINWHEELS

Recipe can be made 3 hours ahead.

1¾ cups (250g) dried figs, chopped
¼ cup orange juice
3 cups self-raising flour
20g polyunsaturated margarine
1 tablespoon grated orange rind
1 cup skim milk
¼ cup water, approximately
ORANGE ICING
1 cup icing sugar
1 teaspoon grated orange rind
2 tablespoons orange juice, approximately

Combine figs and juice in bowl, stand for several hours or overnight.

Lightly grease deep 23cm round cake pan, line base with baking paper. Sift flour into bowl, rub in margarine. Stir in rind and milk with enough water to mix to a firm dough, knead on lightly floured surface until smooth. Roll dough to 20cm x 40cm rectangle.

♥ ♥ ♥

OATY SULTANA BISCUITS

Biscuits can be made 3 days ahead.

1½ cups rolled oats
½ cup sultanas
¼ cup self-raising flour
¼ cup brown sugar
2 egg whites
2 tablespoons honey
**20g polyunsaturated margarine,
    melted**

Combine oats, sultanas, sifted flour and sugar in bowl. Stir in combined egg whites, honey and margarine. Drop heaped tablespoons of mixture about 3cm apart on baking paper covered oven trays, press with fork. Bake in moderate oven for about 15 minutes or until golden brown. Lift onto wire rack to cool.
    Makes 16.
■ Suitable to freeze.
■ Not suitable to microwave.
■ Total fat: 29g.
■ Fat per biscuit: 1.8g.

♥ ♥ ♥

MAPLE SYRUP AND PECAN CAKE

Cake can be made 4 days ahead.

1 cup All-Bran
½ cup brown sugar
1½ cups skim milk
¼ cup water
¾ cup sultanas
¼ cup chopped pecans
½ cup self-raising flour
1 cup wholemeal self-raising flour
2 teaspoons mixed spice

SYRUP
½ cup maple syrup
2 tablespoons water

Lightly grease 14cm x 21cm loaf pan, line base with baking paper. Combine All-Bran, sugar, milk, water, sultanas and nuts in bowl, stand 10 minutes. Stir in sifted flours and spice.
    Spread mixture into prepared pan, bake in moderately slow oven for about 1¼ hours or until firm. Stand cake in pan for 5 minutes, turn onto wire rack; stand rack on tray. Pour hot syrup over cake.
Syrup: Combine syrup and water in pan, stir until hot.
    Serves 10.
■ Suitable to freeze.
■ Not suitable to microwave.
■ Total fat: 28g.
■ Fat per slice: 2.8g.

LEFT: Custard Tarts with Low-Fat Sweet Pastry.
BELOW: Clockwise from back left: Cranberry Muffins, Oaty Sultana Biscuits, Fig and Orange Pinwheels, Maple Syrup and Pecan Cake.

♥ ♥ ♥

BANANA NUT LOAF

You will need 2 large over-ripe bananas. Loaf can be made a day ahead.

¼ cup chopped hazelnuts
¼ cup chopped dates
2¼ cups self-raising flour
⅓ cup brown sugar
1 cup mashed banana
½ cup buttermilk
¼ cup skim milk powder
2 tablespoons corn syrup
2 egg whites

Lightly grease 15cm x 25cm loaf pan, line base with baking paper. Combine nuts, dates, sifted flour and sugar in bowl; stir in banana. Gradually stir in combined buttermilk, skim milk powder, corn syrup and egg whites until combined. Pour mixture into prepared pan. Bake in moderate oven for about 45 minutes or until firm.

Serves 12.

■ Suitable to freeze.
■ Not suitable to microwave.
□ Total fat: 19.4g.
■ Fat per slice: 1.6g.

♥ ♥ ♥

APRICOT PRUNE LOAF

Loaf can be made 2 days ahead.

½ cup dried apricots
1¼ cups water
1 over-ripe banana
2 cups wholemeal self-raising flour
¼ cup castor sugar
½ teaspoon ground cinnamon
30g polyunsaturated margarine
½ cup pitted prunes, chopped
1 egg, lightly beaten

Lightly grease 14cm x 21cm loaf pan, line with baking paper. Combine apricots and water in pan, bring to boil, simmer for 5 minutes; cool to room temperature. Blend or process apricot mixture and banana until smooth.

Sift flour, sugar and cinnamon into bowl, rub in margarine. Stir in prunes, egg and apricot mixture. Spoon mixture into prepared pan, bake in moderate oven for about 45 minutes or until firm. Stand 5 minutes before turning onto wire rack to cool.

Serves 10.
◼ Suitable to freeze.
◼ Not suitable to microwave.
◻ Total fat: 36g.
◼ Fat per slice: 3.6g.

♥ ♥ ♥
APPLE GINGER SHORTCAKE

You will need about 2 passionfruit. Recipe can be made a day ahead.

PASTRY
1¼ cups self-raising flour
1 tablespoon cornflour
2 tablespoons castor sugar
40g polyunsaturated margarine
2 egg whites
1 teaspoon lemon juice,
approximately

APPLE GINGER FILLING
450g can pie apples
1 tablespoon passionfruit pulp
1 teaspoon finely chopped
glace ginger
1 teaspoon grated lemon rind

PASSIONFRUIT ICING
1 cup icing sugar
1 teaspoon polyunsaturated
margarine
1 tablespoon passionfruit pulp
1 teaspoon skim milk, approximately

Pastry: Lightly grease 20cm round sandwich pan, line base with baking paper. Sift dry ingredients into bowl, rub in margarine, stir in egg whites with enough juice to make ingredients cling together (or process all ingredients until mixture forms a ball), cover, refrigerate for 30 minutes.

Roll three-quarters of the pastry between 2 pieces of greaseproof paper until large enough to line base and side of prepared pan. Spread filling over base, fold pastry edge over filling, lightly brush edge with water. Roll out remaining pastry to a 20cm round, place over filling, press edges to seal. Bake in moderate oven for about 40 minutes or until lightly browned. Cool on wire rack. Spread with icing.
Apple Ginger Filling: Combine all ingredients in bowl; mix well.

Passionfruit Icing: Sift icing sugar into heatproof bowl, stir in margarine and passionfruit, then enough milk to make a stiff paste. Stir over hot water until icing is spreadable.

Serves 10.
◻ Not suitable to freeze.
◼ Not suitable to microwave.
◻ Total fat: 43g.
◼ Fat per serve: 4.3g.

LEFT: From top: Banana Nut Loaf, Apricot Prune Loaf.
ABOVE: Apple Ginger Shortcake.

111

♥ ♥ ♥
PEACH AND YOGURT CAKE

Cake is best made just before serving; serve warm.

2 cups wholemeal self-raising flour
½ cup castor sugar
2 teaspoons ground cinnamon
1 teaspoon ground ginger
½ teaspoon ground allspice
1 teaspoon vanilla essence
100g sachet Scramblers
½ cup water
½ cup low-fat plain yogurt
1 tablespoon olive oil
410g can pie peaches

Lightly grease 23cm square cake pan, line base with baking paper. Sift flour, sugar and spices into bowl. Add essence, Scramblers, water, yogurt and oil, beat with electric mixer until smooth.

Reserve quarter of mixture. Spread remaining mixture into prepared pan. Top with peaches, spread with reserved mixture. Bake in moderate oven for about 45 minutes or lightly browned. Stand for 5 minutes before turning onto wire rack to cool.

Serves 12.

■ Suitable to freeze.
■ Not suitable to microwave.
■ Total fat: 36.8g.
■ Fat per serve: 3g.

♥ ♥ ♥
FRUITY COOKIES

Cookies can be made 3 days ahead.

1 cup wholemeal self-raising flour
½ teaspoon ground cinnamon
½ teaspoon ground nutmeg
2 tablespoons brown sugar
1 tablespoon finely chopped
**   dried apricots**
1 tablespoon finely chopped
**   dried apples**
1 tablespoon sultanas
1 tablespoon olive oil
100g sachet Scramblers
¼ cup skim milk

Sift dry ingredients into bowl, stir in fruit; make well in centre. Add oil, Scramblers and milk, stir until combined. Place 2 heaped table-spoons mixture about 5cm apart onto non-stick oven trays. Bake in moderately hot oven for about 15 minutes or until lightly browned; cool on trays.

Makes 8.

■ Suitable to freeze.
■ Not suitable to microwave.
■ Total fat: 33g.
■ Fat per cookie: 4g.

♥ ♥ ♥
APPLE CINNAMON BISCUITS WITH PASSIONFRUIT ICING

You will need about 2 passionfruit. Biscuits can be made 2 weeks ahead.

1 cup self-raising flour
½ teaspoon ground cinnamon
40g polyunsaturated margarine
1 apple, grated
⅓ cup orange juice
½ cup rolled oats
2 tablespoons golden syrup
PASSIONFRUIT ICING
1 cup icing sugar
1 tablespoon passionfruit pulp
1 teaspoon polyunsaturated margarine
1 teaspoon skim milk, approximately

Sift flour and cinnamon into bowl, rub in margarine. Stir in apple, juice, oats and golden syrup. Drop heaped tablespoons of mixture 5cm apart onto non-stick oven tray, bake in moderate oven for about 40 minutes or until lightly browned. Lift biscuits onto wire rack to cool. Spread cold biscuits with passionfruit icing.
Passionfruit Icing: Sift icing sugar into heatproof bowl, stir in passionfruit and margarine, then enough milk to make a stiff paste. Stir over hot water until spreadable.
  Makes 24.
■ Suitable to freeze.
■ Not suitable to microwave.
□ Total fat: 46.6g.
■ Fat per biscuit: 1.9g.

LEFT: Clockwise from back: Peach and Yogurt Cake, Apple Cinnamon Biscuits with Passionfruit Icing, Fruity Cookies.

China from Royal Doulton; table from Appley Hoare Antiques

Drinks

♥ ♥ ♥

PEACH SUNRISE

Prepare drink 3 hours ahead.

⅔ cup boiling water
1 tea bag
425g can peaches
⅓ cup low-fat plain yogurt
2 teaspoons grenadine syrup

Pour boiling water over tea bag in cup, stand for 5 minutes, discard tea bag; cool tea to room temperature; do not refrigerate tea.

Drain peaches, reserve ⅓ cup syrup. Blend or process peaches, reserved syrup, tea and yogurt until smooth. Swirl grenadine into 2 glasses, pour in peach mixture.
Serves 2.
▢ Total fat: Negligible.

LEFT: From left: Honeydew Dream, Peach Sunrise, Pineapple Wine Whip.
ABOVE: Banana Sultana Whip.

Left: Glasses from Village Living

♥ ♥ ♥

HONEYDEW DREAM

Make recipe just before serving.

250g honeydew melon, chopped
1 tablespoon skim milk powder
1 tablespoon lime juice
2 tablespoons buttermilk
1 teaspoon sugar
6 ice cubes

Blend or process all ingredients until smooth and creamy.
Serves 2.
▢ Total fat: Negligible.

♥ ♥ ♥

PINEAPPLE WINE WHIP

Make recipe just before serving.

500g pineapple, chopped
⅓ cup castor sugar
1 cup sweet white wine
3 teaspoons coconut essence
⅓ cup water

Spread pineapple on freezer tray; partially freeze. Blend or process pineapple, sugar, wine, essence and water until smooth.
Serves 4.
▢ Total fat: Negligible.

♥ ♥ ♥

BANANA SULTANA WHIP

Make recipe just before serving.

1 cup skim milk
1 tablespoon lemon juice
1 banana, chopped
2 tablespoons sultanas
2 tablespoons wheatgerm
2 teaspoons golden syrup
¼ teaspoon ground cinnamon

Blend or process all ingredients until smooth and creamy.
Serves 2.
▢ Total fat: 3g.
■ Fat per serve: 1.5g.

♥ ♥ ♥
ICED GINGER COFFEE

Make recipe just before serving.

2 teaspoons dry instant coffee
1 cup boiling water
¾ cup skim milk
¼ cup dry ginger ale

Combine coffee and water in jug; cool, then refrigerate until cold. Stir in remaining ingredients. Serve with ice.
   Serves 2.
   ▢ Total fat: Negligible.

♥ ♥ ♥
MANGO SMOOTHIE

Make recipe just before serving.

1 large mango, chopped
1 cup skim milk
½ cup orange juice
1 tablespoon sugar

Blend or process all ingredients until smooth and creamy.
   Serves 2.
   ▢ Total fat: Negligible.

♥ ♥ ♥
APRICOT TROPICANA

Make recipe just before serving.

425g can apricot halves, drained
1 apple, chopped
1 banana, chopped
1 mango, chopped
1 cup lemonade
1 tablespoon white rum
1 tablespoon gin

Blend or process all ingredients until well combined.
   Serves 4.
   ▢ Total fat: Negligible.

♥ ♥ ♥
TOMATO SPARKLE

Make recipe just before serving.

2 tomatoes, peeled, chopped
1 teaspoon Worcestershire sauce
1 tablespoon sugar
1 tablespoon chopped fresh mint
375ml can mineral water
red food colouring

Blend or process tomatoes, sauce and sugar until well combined. Combine tomato mixture, mint, mineral water in jug. Tint with colouring, if desired.
   Serves 2.
   ▢ Total fat: Negligible.

ABOVE: Iced Ginger Coffee.
RIGHT: From left: Mango Smoothie, Apricot Tropicana, Tomato Sparkle.

Above and right: Glasses from Village Living

10

Layered Vegetable Soy Bean Loaf
Honeyed Chicken Stir-Fry
Triple Rice Salad with Citrus Plum Dressing
Potato Tomato Salad with Garlic Yogurt Cream
Fruit Platter with Redcurrant Sauce
Pavlova with Peach Custard

Your guests will enjoy plenty to eat with these light but satisfying dishes — even 2 luscious desserts! Fat per person is about 9g over all courses.

♥ ♥ ♥

LAYERED VEGETABLE SOY BEAN LOAF

Make recipe just before serving.

**445g can soy beans,
rinsed, drained**
1 cup seasoned stuffing mix
**100g pouch Just White Egg
White Mix**
2 cloves garlic, crushed
½ teaspoon chilli powder
TOPPING
2 carrots, grated
2 zucchini, grated
2 green shallots, chopped
250g pumpkin, grated
2 potatoes, grated
½ cup low-fat cottage cheese
2 x 100g sachets Scramblers
⅓ cup skim milk

Line 14cm x 21cm loaf pan with baking paper. Blend or process beans, stuffing mix, egg white mix, garlic and chilli until well combined. Spread mixture into prepared pan, bake in moderate oven for about 20 minutes or until firm; cool.

Spread topping over loaf in pan, bake in moderate oven for about 30 minutes, or until firm and lightly browned. Serve warm or cold.
Topping: Combine all ingredients in bowl; mix well.

Serves 10.
■ Not suitable to freeze.
■ Not suitable to microwave.
■ Total fat: 43.5g.
■ Fat per serve: 4.4g.

LEFT: Back, from left: Pavlova with Peach Custard, Triple Rice Salad with Citrus Plum Dressing, Potato Tomato Salad with Garlic Yogurt Cream. Front, from left: Fruit Platter with Redcurrant Sauce, Honeyed Chicken Stir-Fry, Layered Vegetable Soy Bean Loaf.

China and cutlery from Dansab

ABOVE: From top: Honeyed Chicken Stir-Fry, Fruit Platter with Redcurrant Sauce.

♥ ♥ ♥
HONEYED CHICKEN STIR-FRY

Cook recipe just before serving.

1¼kg chicken breast fillets, sliced
⅓ cup salt-reduced soy sauce
½ cup honey
2 cloves garlic, crushed
1 teaspoon chopped fresh ginger
1 red pepper, chopped
500g broccoli, chopped
2 x 425g cans baby corn, drained
½ medium cabbage, shredded

Combine chicken, sauce, honey, garlic and ginger in bowl, refrigerate for several hours or overnight.

Cook mixture in non-stick pan or wok until chicken is tender; remove mixture from pan. Add pepper, broccoli and corn to pan, stir-fry for about 5 minutes or until broccoli is just tender. Stir in chicken and cabbage, stir until cabbage is just wilted.

Serves 10.
■ Not suitable to freeze.
■ Not suitable to microwave.
■ Total fat: 27g.
■ Fat per serve: 2.7g.

♥ ♥ ♥

TRIPLE RICE SALAD WITH CITRUS PLUM DRESSING

Recipe can be made a day ahead. Salad can be served hot or cold.

1½ cups (290g) wild rice
2 litres (8 cups) water
5 yellow zucchini, sliced
1½ cups (290g) brown rice
2 cups frozen peas
2 carrots
1 cup basmati rice
CITRUS PLUM DRESSING
¼ cup lemon juice
2 tablespoons lime juice
⅓ cup orange juice
2 teaspoons sambal oelek
1 teaspoon polyunsaturated oil
2 tablespoons plum jam, sieved
¼ cup chopped fresh chives

Combine wild rice with 3 cups of the water in pan, bring to boil, simmer, covered, for about 20 minutes or until rice is tender and almost all liquid is absorbed. Stir in zucchini, cook, covered, further 5 minutes or until all liquid is absorbed. Stir in one-third of the dressing.

Combine brown rice with 3 cups of the remaining water in pan, bring to boil, simmer, covered, for about 20 minutes or until rice is tender and almost all liquid is absorbed. Stir in peas, cook, covered, further 5 minutes or until all liquid is absorbed. Stir in half the remaining dressing.

Cut carrots into thin strips. Combine basmati rice with remaining water in pan, bring to boil, simmer, covered, for about 12 minutes or until rice is tender and almost all liquid is absorbed. Stir in carrots, cook, covered, for about 5 minutes or until all liquid is absorbed. Stir in remaining dressing; mix well.
Citrus Plum Dressing: Blend or process juices, sambal oelek, oil and jam until smooth; stir in chives.
 Serves 10.
■ Not suitable to freeze.
■ Not suitable to microwave.
□ Total fat: 11.8g.
■ Fat per serve: 1.2g.

♥ ♥ ♥

POTATO TOMATO SALAD WITH GARLIC YOGURT CREAM

Recipe can be made a day ahead. Salad can be served warm or cold.

2kg baby potatoes, halved
2 x 250g punnets cherry tomatoes
GARLIC YOGURT CREAM
2 tablespoons skim milk powder
⅓ cup low-fat plain yogurt
⅓ cup buttermilk
2 tablespoons no-added-salt tomato paste
2 tablespoons lemon juice
2 tablespoons chopped fresh flat-leafed parsley
2 tablespoons chopped fresh basil
2 cloves garlic, crushed

Boil, steam or microwave potatoes until tender; drain. Combine potatoes and tomatoes in serving bowl; add dressing just before serving.
Garlic Yogurt Cream: Blend or process skim milk powder, yogurt, buttermilk, paste and juice until smooth. Stir in herbs and garlic.
 Serves 10.
■ Not suitable to freeze.
■ Suitable to microwave.
□ Total fat: 1.5g.
■ Fat per serve: Negligible.

♥ ♥ ♥

FRUIT PLATTER WITH REDCURRANT SAUCE

You will need about 6 passionfruit for this recipe. Fruit is best prepared close to serving time. Sauce can be made a day ahead.

2 mangoes, sliced
2 x 250g punnets strawberries
½ rockmelon, sliced
4 oranges, segmented
2 pears, sliced
2 apples, sliced
2 bananas, sliced
6 kiwi fruit, sliced
250g punnet blueberries
½ cup passionfruit pulp
REDCURRANT SAUCE
200g fresh or frozen redcurrants
1½ cups water
¼ cup sugar
1 tablespoon cornflour
1 tablespoon water, extra
2 tablespoons Grand Marnier

Arrange fruit on serving platter; serve with sauce.
Redcurrant Sauce: Combine redcurrants, water and sugar in pan, bring to boil, simmer, covered, for 3 minutes. Blend or process mixture until smooth, strain; discard seeds. Return liquid to pan, stir in blended cornflour and extra water, stir until sauce boils and thickens. Stir in liqueur.
 Serves 10.
■ Not suitable to freeze.
■ Suitable to microwave.
□ Total fat: Negligible.

♥ ♥ ♥

PAVLOVA WITH PEACH CUSTARD

Pavlova and custard can be made a day ahead. Assemble pavlova 3 hours before serving.

6 egg whites
1½ cups castor sugar
PEACH CUSTARD
½ cup castor sugar
½ cup cornflour
¼ cup custard powder
2¼ cups skim milk
3 x 425g cans peaches in natural juice, drained

Mark 28cm circle on baking paper-covered oven tray. Beat egg whites in large bowl with electric mixer until soft peaks form. Gradually add sugar, beat until dissolved between each addition.

Spread half the egg white mixture over circle on tray, pipe remaining mixture around edge. Bake in very slow oven for about 1½ hours or until dry to touch. Turn oven off; cool pavlova in oven with door ajar.

Fill cold pavlova with custard; decorate with extra peaches, if desired.
Peach Custard: Combine sugar, cornflour and custard powder in pan, gradually stir in milk. Stir over heat until custard boils and thickens, simmer for 1 minute; cool. Blend or process peaches and custard until smooth.
 Serves 10.
■ Not suitable to freeze.
■ Not suitable to microwave.
□ Total fat: Negligible.

Easy Dinner Party for 6

MENU
Jellied Beetroot with Chive Dressing
Lamb Noisettes with Leek and Pepper Sauce
Mixed Green Salad
Sorbet Pastry Rings with Butterscotch Sauce

Both the entree and the dessert
are made ahead, leaving you
only the main course to prepare just
before serving. Fat per person
is about 18g over all courses.

♥ ♥ ♥
JELLIED BEETROOT WITH CHIVE DRESSING

Recipe can be made a day ahead.

400g fresh beetroot
1 cup orange juice
1 cup cranberry jelly
1 tablespoon gelatine
2 tablespoons water
CHIVE DRESSING
1 tablespoon polyunsaturated oil
1 tablespoon lemon juice
2 teaspoons white wine vinegar
2 teaspoons chopped fresh chives
¼ teaspoon cracked black peppercorns
¼ teaspoon seeded mustard

Wash beetroot, cut off leafy tops. Cook beetroot in pan of boiling water for about 1 hour or until skin can be removed easily; drain. Remove skin; chop beetroot finely.

Heat juice and jelly in pan, stir until jelly is dissolved. Sprinkle gelatine over water in cup, stand in small pan of simmering water, stir until dissolved. Stir gelatine into juice mixture; stir in beetroot. Pour into 6 wetted moulds (½ cup capacity), refrigerate for several hours or overnight until set. Unmould jellies onto plates, serve with chive dressing.

Chive Dressing: Combine all ingredients in jar; shake well.
Serves 6.
■ Not suitable to freeze.
■ Not suitable to microwave.
▢ Total fat: 18g.
■ Fat per serve: 3g.

LEFT: Clockwise from front: Jellied Beetroot with Chive Dressing, Mixed Green Salad, Sorbet Pastry Rings with Butterscotch Sauce, Lamb Noisettes with Leek and Pepper Sauce.

China from Villeroy & Boch

♥ ♥
LAMB NOISETTES
WITH LEEK AND PEPPER SAUCE

Cook noisettes just before serving. Sauce can be made 3 hours ahead.

12 x 80g lamb noisettes
½ cup cooked brown rice
4 green shallots, chopped
2 teaspoons chopped fresh thyme

LEEK AND PEPPER SAUCE
1 tablespoon oil
1 leek, sliced
1 carrot, finely chopped
1 red pepper, chopped
1 vegetable stock cube, crumbled
2 cups water
1 tablespoon chopped fresh mint
1 teaspoon chopped fresh thyme
2 green shallots, chopped
3 teaspoons cornflour
¼ cup water, extra

Trim all visible fat from noisettes. Cut a deep pocket in top of each noisette. Combine rice, shallots and thyme in bowl. Fill pockets with rice mixture, secure with toothpicks. Grill noisettes until tender. Serve with sauce.

Leek and Pepper Sauce: Heat oil in pan, add leek, stir over heat until leek is soft. Stir in carrot, pepper, combined stock cube and water, bring to boil, simmer, covered, for about 7 minutes or until vegetables are tender. Stir in herbs, shallots and blended cornflour and extra water. Stir over heat until sauce boils and thickens.

Serves 6.
◻ Not suitable to freeze.
◼ Lamb not suitable to microwave.
◻ Total fat: 55.4g.
◼ Fat per serve: 9.3g.

♥ ♥ ♥
MIXED GREEN SALAD

Make recipe just before serving.

2 zucchini, chopped
250g bunch fresh asparagus, chopped
6 cups (½ bunch) torn curly endive leaves
3 cups (¼ bunch) watercress sprigs
1 radicchio lettuce
DRESSING
1 cup No Oil French dressing
1 tablespoon olive oil
2 tablespoons chopped fresh tarragon
½ teaspoon cracked black peppercorns
½ teaspoon sugar
2 teaspoons seeded mustard
1 tablespoon no-added-salt tomato paste

Boil, steam or microwave zucchini and asparagus until just tender, rinse under cold water; drain. Combine all vegetables in bowl, add dressing.
Dressing: Combine all ingredients in bowl; mix well.

Serves 6.
◻ Total fat: 18g.
◼ Fat per serve: 3g.

♥ ♥ ♥
SORBET PASTRY RINGS
WITH BUTTERSCOTCH SAUCE

Recipe can be made 3 days ahead.

2 teaspoons polyunsaturated margarine
1 cup water
⅔ cup self-raising flour
4 egg whites, lightly beaten
ORANGE SORBET
2 cups water
2 tablespoons sugar
⅓ cup lemon juice
1⅓ cups concentrated orange juice
2 egg whites
BUTTERSCOTCH SAUCE
1 cup brown sugar, lightly packed
⅓ cup skim milk
2 teaspoons polyunsaturated margarine

Combine margarine and water in pan, bring to boil. Add sifted flour all at once. Stir vigorously over heat until smooth. Place in small bowl of electric mixer. Add egg whites gradually, beat on low speed after each addition. Mixture will separate, but will come together with further beating.

Spoon mixture into piping pag fitted with 1½cm plain tube. Pipe 6 x 10cm circles of mixture onto baking paper-covered oven tray. Bake in hot oven for 10 minutes, reduce heat to moderate, bake further 15 minutes or until well browned; cool. When pastry rings are cold, cut in half, scoop out any uncooked mixture; discard.

Fill pastry rings with sorbet, freeze until firm. Serve with warm sauce and extra fruit, if desired.
Orange Sorbet: Combine water, sugar and lemon juice in pan, stir over heat until sugar is dissolved. Bring to boil, simmer, uncovered, without stirring, for 2 minutes. Stir in orange juice; pour into freezer tray, cover, freeze until just beginning to set. Stir sorbet with fork in bowl until mushy. Beat egg whites in small bowl until soft peaks form, fold into sorbet.
Butterscotch Sauce: Combine sugar, milk and margarine in pan, bring to boil, boil for 1 minute.

Serves 6.
◻ Suitable to freeze.
◼ Not suitable to microwave.
◻ Total fat: 16.7g.
◼ Fat per serve: 2.8g.

BELOW: Jellied Beetroot with Chive Dressing.

Glossary

Some terms, names and alternatives are included here to help everyone to understand and use our recipes perfectly.

Alcohol. is optional but gives a particular flavour. You can use fruit juice or water instead to make up the liquid content in our recipes.

All-Bran. a low-fat, high-fibre breakfast cereal based on wheat bran.

Allspice. pimento in ground form.

Arrowroot. is made from a combination of starchy extracts from the roots of various tropical plants; it is used mostly for thickening. Cornflour can be substituted.

Baking paper. has a non-stick coating which eliminates the need to grease the paper.

Baking powder. raising agent made from an alkali and acid. It is mostly made from cream of tartar and bicarbonate of soda in the proportion of 1 level teaspoon cream of tartar to ½ level teaspoon bicarbonate of soda. This is equal to 2 level teaspoons baking powder.

Baking ware, non-stick. the surface of oven trays, cake pans, muffin pans, etc, is treated so baked goods turn out easily without greasing.

Barley, rolled. grains are rolled flat, similar to rolled oats.

Beans
Black: fermented, salted soy beans. Use either canned or dried. Drain and rinse the canned variety, soak and rinse the dried variety. Leftover beans will keep for months in the refrigerator. Mash beans when cooking to release flavour.
Black-eyed: also known as black-eyed peas.
Green: French beans.
Mexicana chilli: canned pinto beans with chilli flavouring; several brands are available.

Beef
Blade steak: cut from the forequarter.
Chuck steak: cut from the forequarter.
Scotch fillet: rib eye steak.
Topside steak: cut from the hindquarter.

Bok choy (Chinese chard). discard stems, use leaves and young tender parts of stems. It requires only a short cooking time.

Bran, unprocessed. the outer husk of wheat.

Bread
Pita pocket: unleavened bread which puffs up during cooking, leaving a hollow in the centre.
Wholemeal: we used wholewheat sliced bread.

Breadcrumbs
Packaged: commercially packaged crumbs.
Stale: we used 1- or 2-day-old white or wholemeal bread made into crumbs by grating, blending or processing.

Burghul (cracked wheat). has been cracked by boiling then re-dried.

Cheese
Light mozzarella: we used Reduced Fat Mozzarella Cheese by Kraft Light Naturals.
Low-fat cottage: soft, fresh white cheese made from skim milk.
Reduced-fat ricotta: a low-fat, fresh, unripened cheese made from whey obtained in the manufacture of other cheese.
Reduced-fat tasty: natural cheddar cheese.
Parmesan: very hard cheese available grated or by the piece.

Chick peas. garbanzos when canned.

Chicken
Breast fillet: skinless and boneless.
Drumstick: leg.
Thigh fillet: skinless and boneless.

Chillies, fresh. are available in many types and sizes. The small ones (bird's eye or bird peppers) are the hottest. Use tight-fitting gloves when handling the chopped fresh chillies as they can burn your skin. The seeds are the hottest part, so remove them if you want to reduce the heat content of recipe.

Chilli powder. the Asian variety is the hottest and is made from ground red chillies; it can be used as a substitute for fresh chillies in the proportion of ½ teaspoon ground chilli powder to 1 medium chilli.

Coleslaw dressing. low-oil creamy product.

Cornflour. cornstarch.

Cornmeal (polenta). made from ground corn.

Couscous. a fine cereal made from semolina.

Cream, sour light. a light, commercially cultured sour cream.

Custard powder. pudding mix.

Eggplant. aubergine.

Essence. extract.
Coffee and chicory: a slightly bitter syrup based on sugar, caramel, coffee and chicory.
Vanilla: we used imitation essence.

Flour
Buckwheat: flour milled from buckwheat.
White plain: all-purpose flour.
White self-raising: substitute plain (all purpose) flour and baking powder in the proportion of ¾ metric cup plain flour to 2 level metric teaspoons baking powder, sift together several times before using. If using an 8oz measuring cup, use 1 cup white plain flour to 2 level metric teaspoons baking powder.
Wholemeal plain: wholewheat flour without the addition of baking powder.
Wholemeal self-raising: wholewheat self-raising flour; add baking powder as above to make wholemeal self-raising flour.

Framboise. raspberry-flavoured liqueur.

Garam masala. varied combinations of cardamom, cinnamon, cloves, coriander, cumin and nutmeg make this spice which is often used in Indian cooking. Sometimes pepper is used to make a hot variation. Garam masala is available in jars from Asian food stores and specialty stores.

Ginger
Fresh, green or root: scrape away skin and it is ready to grate, chop or slice.
Glace: ginger which has been cooked in a heavy sugar syrup, then dried. Crystallised ginger can be substituted for glace ginger; rinse off sugar with water, dry before using.

Grand Marnier. an orange-flavoured liqueur.

Greasing. we used a commercial non-stick spray such as Pure and Simple to grease pans.

Herbs. we have specified when to use fresh, ground or dried herbs. We used dried (not ground) herbs in the proportion of 1:4 for fresh herbs — e.g., 1 teaspoon dried herbs instead of 4 teaspoons chopped fresh herbs.

Just White Egg White Mix. a yolk-free, frozen egg substitute available in 300g packets containing 3 pouches. Each pouch is equivalent to the whites of 3 large eggs.

Kumara. an orange-coloured sweet potato.

Lamb
Chump chops: cut from the chump section, between leg and mid-loin.
Fillets: very small, lean, tender cut.

Lentils. there are many types; all require soaking before cooking, except for red lentils which are ready for cooking without soaking.

Mayonnaise, light. use a low oil product.

Melon, honeydew. an oval melon with delicate taste and pale green flesh.

Milk
Buttermilk: the liquid left after cream is separated from milk. It is now made by adding culture to skim milk to give a slightly acid flavour. Use skim milk if unavailable.
Skim milk: milk from which the butterfat has been almost completely removed.
Skim milk powder: has minimal butterfat.

Noodles, egg. are generally sold in compressed bundles and have usually been pre-cooked by steaming so they need only minimal preparation at home.

Oats, rolled. oats have the husks ground off and are then steam-softened and rolled flat.

Oil
Olive: ripe olives are pressed to obtain olive oil. The best oil comes from the first pressing. Two types are marketed, "virgin" and "pure".
Polyunsaturated: edible vegetable oil.

Peppers. capsicum or bell peppers.

Pimientos. sweet red peppers preserved in brine in cans or jars.

Polenta. known as cornmeal or maizemeal; ground from Indian corn.

Polyunsaturated margarine. made from polyunsaturated fats found in vegetable oils. Flavourings, colours and vitamins A and D are usually added.

Pork
Butterfly steak: skinless, boneless mid-loin chop which has been split and opened out flat.
Fillet: skinless, boneless eye-fillet from the loin.
Medallion: eye of the loin.

Pumpkin. any type of pumpkin can be substituted for butternut or golden nugget.

Rice. can be brown or white.
Basmati: a delicately flavoured rice from Pakistan; white long grain rice can be substituted.
Red: a long-grain type of rice with red husks available from Asian food stores.
Rice cake: a gluten and wheat-free product. Rice cakes are a light and crunchy wholegrain crispbread made from rice, corn and water.
Wild: from North America but is not a member of the rice family; it is expensive as it is difficult to cultivate but has a distinctive flavour.

Sauce
Chilli: we used a hot Chinese variety. It consists of chillies, salt and vinegar. We used it sparingly so that you can easily increase the

amounts in recipes to suit your taste.

Cranberry: is cranberries preserved in sugar syrup; has an astringent flavour.

Fish: this sauce is an essential ingredient in the cooking of a number of South-East Asian countries, including Thailand and Vietnam. It is made from the liquid drained from salted, fermented anchovies. It has a strong smell and taste. Use sparingly until you acquire the taste.

Oyster: a rich, brown bottled sauce made from oysters cooked in salt and soy sauce.

Soy: is made from fermented soy beans. The light variety is generally used with white meat dishes, and the darker variety with red meat dishes. The dark is generally used for colour, and the light for flavour.

Sweet chilli: a piquant mix of sugar, chilli, vinegar, salt and spices. Use sparingly.

Tabasco: made with vinegar, hot red peppers and salt. Use sparingly.

Tomato: tomato ketchup; we used a variety with no added salt.

Sambal oelek, also spelt ulek and olek; is a paste made from chillies and salt; use as an ingredient or accompaniment.

Scramblers, a yolk-free, frozen egg substitute available in packets containing 6 x 100g sachets. Each sachet is equivalent to approximately 2 eggs.

Segmenting, cutting citrus fruits in such a way that the pieces contain no pith, seed or membrane. The thickly peeled fruit is cut towards the centre inside each membrane, forming wedges.

Semolina, a cereal made from the endosperm of hard durum wheat. Used in puddings, cakes, desserts and some savoury dishes.

Shallots, green, known as spring onions in some Australian States, scallions in some other countries. Do not confuse with the small golden shallots.

Snow peas, also known as mange-tout, sugar peas or Chinese peas; are small flat pods with tiny, barely formed peas inside; they are eaten whole, pod and all. They require only a short cooking time.

Spice, Chinese assorted, packaged mixed spices available from Asian food stores.

Spinach
English: a soft-leafed vegetable, more delicate in taste than silverbeet (spinach); young, tender silverbeet leaves can be substituted for English spinach.
Silverbeet: a large-leafed vegetable; remove coarse white stems, cook green leafy parts.

Stock cube, 1 small stock cube is equivalent to 1 teaspoon powdered bouillon; 1 large stock cube is equivalent to 2 teaspoons bouillon. These are approximate guides.

Stuffing mix, seasoned, a tasty packaged mix containing breadcrumbs and flavourings.

Sultanas, dried seedless grapes also known as white raisins.

Sugar
Castor: fine granulated table sugar.
Crystal: coarse granulated table sugar.
Icing: confectioners' sugar.

Syrup
Corn: an imported product available in supermarkets, delicatessens and health food stores. It is available in light or dark; either can be substituted for the other.
Golden: a by-product of sugar; honey can usually be substituted.
Grenadine: non-alcoholic flavouring made from pomegranate juice; bright red in colour. Imitation cordial is also available.
Maple: we used Grade A Dark Amber Maple Syrup; it is an imported product. Pancake syrup, golden syrup or honey can usually be substituted.

Tahini paste, is made from crushed sesame seeds; is widely used as a flavouring in Middle Eastern and Latin American cookery.

Tangerines, a variety of mandarin with deeper, orange-red skin which is easily peeled; generally very sweet and juicy.

Tempeh, is produced by a natural culture of soy beans; has a chunky, chewy texture.

Toasting, almonds and shredded coconut can be toasted in the oven. Spread them evenly onto an oven tray, toast in moderate oven for about 5 minutes. Desiccated coconut and sesame seeds toast more evenly by stirring over heat in a heavy dry pan. The natural oils will brown these ingredients.

Tofu, is made from boiled, crushed soy beans to give a type of milk. A coagulant is added, much like the process of cheese making. We used soft tofu and firm tofu. Tofu is easily digested, nutritious and has a slightly nutty flavour. Buy it as fresh as possible; keep any leftover tofu in the refrigerator under water, which must be changed daily.

Tomato
Paste: a concentrated tomato puree used in flavouring soups, stews, sauces, etc. We used a variety with no added salt.
Puree: is canned pureed tomatoes.
Tomatoes, canned: we used a variety with no added salt.

Veal
Nut of veal: a solid piece of meat off the leg.
Medallion: eye of the loin.

Vermouth, a wine flavoured with a number of different herbs and generally used as an aperitif and cocktails.

Vinegar
Cider vinegar: made from fermented apples.
Red wine vinegar: is made from red wine by a slow process, flavoured with herbs and spices; it has strong aromatic qualities.
White wine vinegar: made from white wine, flavoured with herbs, spices and fruit.

Wholemeal, wholewheat.

Wine, we used good quality dry red and dry white wines. For a sweet white wine in a dessert, we used a moselle.
Green ginger wine: an Australian sweet white wine infused with crushed fresh ginger.

Wrappers
Gow gee wrappers or pastry: are sold frozen, thaw before using; keep covered with a damp cloth while using.
Spring roll wrappers or pastry: are sold frozen, thaw before using; keep covered with a damp cloth while using.

Yeast, allow 3 teaspoons (7g) dried granulated yeast to 15g compressed (fresh) yeast.

Yogurt, low-fat plain, unflavoured yogurt.

Zucchini, courgette.

OVEN TEMPERATURES

Electric Temperatures	Celsius	Fahrenheit	Gas Temperatures	Celsius	Fahrenheit
Very slow	120	250	Very slow	120	250
Slow	150	300	Slow	150	300
Moderately slow	160-180	325-350	Moderately slow	160	325
Moderate	180-200	375-400	Moderate	180	350
Moderately hot	210-230	425-450	Moderately hot	190	375
Hot	240-250	475-500	Hot	200	400
Very hot	260	525-550	Very hot	230	450

CUP AND SPOON MEASURES

Recipes in this book use this standard metric equipment approved by Standards Australia:
(a) 250 millilitre cup for measuring liquids. A litre jug (capacity 4 cups) is also available.
(b) a graduated set of four cups — measuring 1 cup, half, third and quarter cup — for items such as flour, sugar, etc. When measuring in these fractional cups, level off at the brim.
(c) a graduated set of four spoons; tablespoon (20 millilitre liquid capacity), teaspoon (5 millilitre) half and quarter teaspoons. The Australian, British and American teaspoon each has 5ml capacity.

APPROXIMATE CUP AND SPOON CONVERSION CHART

Australian	American & British	Australian	American & British
1 cup	1¼ cups	⅓ cup	½ cup
¾ cup	1 cup	¼ cup	⅓ cup
⅔ cup	¾ cup	2 tablespoons	¼ cup
½ cup	⅔ cup	1 tablespoon	3 teaspoons

MICROWAVE OVENS

Our recipes have been tested in ovens which vary in output between 600 and 700 watts.

**ALL SPOON MEASUREMENTS ARE LEVEL.
WE HAVE USED LARGE EGGS WITH AN AVERAGE WEIGHT OF 61g EACH
IN ALL RECIPES.**

Index